LEARNING
SUPPORT
SERVICES

Please return
on or before
the last date
stamped below

City College
NORWICH

2 2 APR 2004

INTOLERABLE CRUELTY

story by

Robert Ramsey & Matthew Stone
and
John Romano

screenplay by

Robert Ramsey & Matthew Stone
and
Ethan Coen & Joel Coen

faber and faber

First published in the United Kingdom in 2003
by Faber and Faber Limited
3 Queen Square, London WC1N 3AU

Typeset by Country Setting, Kingsdown, Kent CT14 8ES
Printed in England by Mackays of Chatham plc, Chatham, Kent

Robert Ramsay & Matthew Stone and Ethan Coen & Joel Coen
are hereby identified as authors of this work in accordance with
Section 77 of the Copyright, Designs and Patents Act 1988

A CIP record for this book
is available from the British Library

ISBN 0–571–22165–3

2 4 6 8 10 9 7 5 3 1

Intolerable Cruelty

Universal Pictures and Imagine Entertainment present

INTOLERABLE CRUELTY

MAIN CAST

MILES MASSEY	George Clooney
MARYLIN REXROTH	Catherine Zeta-Jones
DONAVAN DONALY	Geoffrey Rush
HOWARD DOYLE	Billy Bob Thornton
GUS PETCH	Cedric the Entertainer
WRIGLEY	Paul Adelstein
REX REXROTH	Edward Herrmann
BONNIE DONALY	Stacey Travis
SARAH SORKIN	Julia Duffy
RAMONA BARCELONA	Mia Cottet
WHEEZY JOE	Irwin Keyes

MAIN CREW

Directed by	Joel Coen
Written by	Robert Ramsay & Matthew Stone and Ethan Coen & Joel Coen
Story by	Robert Ramsay & Matthew Stone
Produced by	Ethan Coen, Brian Grazer
Executive Producers	James Jacks, Sean Daniel
Cinematography	Roger Deakins
Editing	Roderick Jaynes
Production Design	Leslie McDonald
Music	Carter Burwell

STREET

A man in shades.

His sunglasses and the windshield of the car he drives reflect palm trees flashing by on either side. He is well dressed, in his early forties, with a little rat ponytail.

He slows in front of a swank Beverly Hills home.

A beat-up panel van is parked in the driveway.

The man pulls into the driveway, stops under the carport and gets out.

At the front door of the house he pauses to finger an ad slipped over the doorknob: OLLIE'LL FIX IT.

INT. DONALY HOUSE

A fountain gurgles in the tiled front foyer.

> MAN

Bonnie!

After a beat we hear a distant and surprised:

> BONNIE

. . . Donovan?

Donovan glances over to the side. Promotional literature – OLLIE'LL FIX IT *– is stacked on the floor.*

We follow as the man walks toward the voice. He turns a corner down a hallway. A door at the end of the hall is just closing. An adjacent door stands open.

> DONOVAN

. . . Bonnie?

> BONNIE
> (*still distant*)

. . . Donovan.

Donovan scowls and, reaching the end of the hall, glances in the open door.

It is an empty bedroom, its bed rumpled.

Donovan tries the door at the end of the hall. It is locked.

> DONOVAN

Bonnie?

> BONNIE

Yes . . .

The voice is coming from the open bedroom; Donovan enters.

BEDROOM

Bonnie is just emerging from a walk-in closet, straightening her dress.

> BONNIE

Donovan – is everything all right?

> DONOVAN

Yeah, the production meeting was put off so I thought I'd – who's here?

> BONNIE

Here?

> DONOVAN

Mm, what's – whose piece of shit van out front?

> BONNIE

No, uh, nothing, just a guy selling, uh . . . pool cleaner.

> DONOVAN

Why'd he lock himself in the den?

> BONNIE

Well, he, uh . . .

Miserable, she slowly brings out:

Oh God . . . Remember my friend . . . Ollie?

> DONOVAN

Yeah. Yeah. Ollie, right. Of course. Ollie Olerud. Tall, foolish-looking wanker.

Bonnie grimaces and indicates the next room with a jerk of the head. Donovan is surprised.

Ollie *is in there?*

BONNIE
Yes, for Christ's sake, Donovan.

DONOVAN
With the pool cleaner?

BONNIE
Donovan, please. Just Ollie.

DONOVAN
Oh, I see. Well, I'm glad he finally got a job. Always pegged him for a deadbeat. Happy to be proved wrong. Selling pool cleaner now, huh? Well, this would be the neighborhood for it. Just door-to-door, 'Running low on chlorine?', that kind of thing? Quite a coincidence, what, him stopping by here, and you two knowing each other –

BONNIE
Donovan, please –

The den door clicks open. Bonnie and Donovan stop short.

Ollie Olerud, a big shambling blond man with a wispy beard, emerges.

OLLIE
Heya Donovan, how ya doin', man?

DONOVAN
Good, Ollie, and yourself?

Donovan crosses to a bureau and starts rummaging.

OLLIE
Can't complain, man.

DONOVAN
Excellent. Let's get to it then, shall we? We'll take a couple of vacuum hoses and we probably also need a new filter 'round now or – wait a minute . . . Darling, do we *have* a swimming pool?

Okay, man, let's be reasonable about this. Okay, so I had relations with your old lady, so we're all a little embarrassed and, what the fuck, man, I know it's a drag and, ya know, a guy's gotta, I mean these things happen –

Donovan turns from the bureau with a gun.

Ollie takes a step back.

. . . Hey man, I was just kidding about the – we didn't actually have *sex* . . . I was depressed, ya know, I've uh . . . I've been impotent, ya know, unable to achieve an erection for about a year and I had to talk to someone about it . . .

He is slowly backing out the door.

I mean, a year without an erection – think about it, man . . .

Donovan raises the gun but is struck violently from behind by Bonnie, with the pedestal end of a large trophy.

Ollie has disappeared. We hear his footsteps racing down the hallway and his receding voice:

Jesus, man . . .

Donovan is stooping to retrieve the gun that he dropped with the blow.

DONOVAN

Sodding sods . . . bloody sodding –

BONNIE

Leave him alone!

She hits him again with the trophy.

DONOVAN

Ooof!

BONNIE

You should've seen this coming, you insensitive shit!

Donovan straightens painfully, hand to his head.

DONOVAN

You vicious bitch! That's my Daytime Television Lifetime Achievement Award!

Bonnie grabs the trophy by the base. The trophy consists of a gleaming human form of indeterminate sex holding high a sword. She swings the trophy back.

BONNIE
You cheesy bastard!

She stabs him in the thigh with the spiked top of the award, and runs out the door.

Donovan bellows:

DONOVAN
Coo bloody Christ! You whore!

He picks up the trophy and hobbles over to a closet and flings it open.

From out front we hear the horrible wheezing kashl kashl *of the panel van trying to turn over.*

. . . All right, we'll play it that way . . .

He is furiously flinging things from the closet shelves to the floor, searching for something.

. . . You want bloody games? Good then! We'll do bloody games then!

He turns from the closet empty-handed.

. . . Sodding fun and games, you tart? . . .

We still hear the wheezing kashl *of the panel van, and now another car, honking at it.*

Donovan starts emptying another closet, flinging tennis rackets, rollerblades and other impedimenta of Beverly Hills living to the floor.

DONOVAN
Bloody evidence, you bitch! Explain this away . . .

He turns away clutching a Polaroid camera and hobbles frantically to the room's front window just as we hear the van roaring to life over the furiously blaring car horn.

Donovan raises the camera to his eye just as the van is thrown into gear. Lurching into a hard U, the van exposes its other side bearing a stencilled OLLIE'LL FIX IT.

7

Explain this away!

Snap! The flash goes off, sheeting the window and blinding him.

Blast!

The van is barrelling out of the driveway.

Donovan takes his gun out and fires furiously at the window, which shatters, as we see a shrieking Jaguar peel out of the drive, which is now cleared of the van.

Sodding bitch! My bloody Jag!

Thrown off-balance by the gunplay and his gammy leg, Donovan hops around briefly, waving the gun with one arm and the Polaroid camera with the other.

He throws the gun to the floor and sits heavily, his bad leg sticking out in front of him.

Explain this away, you painted harlot!

He is taking pictures of his own leg now, and then of the bloody trophy on the floor next to it.

He chuckles to himself, Ben Gunn-like, taking snap after snap, the photos feeding with a whir out of the front of the camera and plopping into his lap.

Sodding fun and games? We'll see . . . We'll see . . .

Fade out.

In black: the whine of the Polaroid feed-out blends with an intermittent, higher-pitched whine. Presentation credits play in the black and then head titles play over the following:

BRITE SMILE OFFICE

Hanging dental instruments.

Beyond them we see a window showing tops of palm trees. The high-pitched whine ends and a hand reaches in to hang a tooth polisher from the circular instrument rack.

We cut to white teeth. Their owner is talking:

> TEETH
>
> . . . It's me, any messages? . . . Yeah? . . . Just polishing.
> What else?

*Lips draw back as the high-speed whine resumes and a spinning
dental polisher enters to buff the teeth. A brief once-over and the
polisher withdraws.*

> . . . Okay, tell Amstedler I'll return in twenty minutes, have
> Wrigley look up Oliphant vee Oliphant Commonwealth of
> Virginia for its relevance to the Chapman filing, and – wait
> – she took the kids to Tahoe? . . .

CAR

*We are looking through the windshield. We are close on the driver, but
reflections – the windshield-bent image of passing palm trees curving
up into a bright-blue sky – obscure everything except the driver's teeth.*

> TEETH
>
> Which side of Tahoe? . . . Great: if the cruise goes all the
> way around the lake she left the state and she's in breach;
> tell Wrigley to prepare a filing to attach . . . Everything!
> Primary residence, beach house, ski cabin, autos, stocks,
> bonds, dental floss –

*The car turns and bumps and the blue sky in the windshield is
abruptly wiped away by bent overhead fluorescents.*

> – Gonna lose you!

LAW OFFICE CORRIDOR

*A secretary. She is wearing a phone headset, sitting in an outer-office
cubicle. After the briefest phone chirp:*

> SECRETARY
>
> Uh-huh.

The familiar voice, now phone-filtered:

TEETH

. . . And tell Fred Armatrading that we finally have pictures of his wife with the tennis pro. Oh! – and we'll need a fruit-and-pastry basket for the conference room for my nine-thirty – I didn't have time for breakfast this morning.

SECRETARY

Where are you?

The line clicks to dial tone and we hear an approaching voice:

TEETH

Coming atcha.

The teeth arrive, with their owner: Miles Massey, suave, successful, and well groomed.

SECRETARY

Your nine o'clock is here: Bonnie Donaly.

Miles is passing her desk but comes up short. He reaches down to her compact, lying on the desktop, and tilts up its mirror and bares his teeth at it.

MILES

Bonnie Donaly.

He grabs the doorknob to the inner office, puts on a smile, and swings it open.

. . . Mrs Donaly!

He enters and swings the door closed, into the lens.

MILES'S OFFICE

The office is nicely appointed: you probably saw it in last month's World of Interiors. *Massey sits tilted back behind his desk, gazing at the ceiling. In front of the desk sits Bonnie Donaly, the wife from the first scene.*

MILES

Mm. Yes. Your husband did show remarkable foresight in taking those pictures. And yes, absent a swimming pool, the presence of the pool man would appear to be suspicious. But madam, who is the real victim here? Let me suggest the following. Your husband, who on a prior occasion had slapped you – *beat* you, I think that word is not inappropriate –

BONNIE

But I –

MILES

Let me finish. Please. I'm not interested in who slapped whom first. Your husband, who has beaten you – repeatedly –

BONNIE

He –

MILES

Please! – repeatedly, was at the time brandishing your firearm –

BONNIE

It's *his* gun.

MILES

– and we'll get it back for you! – brandishing a firearm, trying in his rage to shoot an acquaintance – a friend of long standing –

BONNIE

They never really cared for each other.

MILES

So he says now! – an old friend and, but for your cool-headed intervention, his tantrum might have ended this shmoe's life – and ruined his own. As for the sexual indiscretion which he imagined had taken place, wasn't it in fact *he* who had been sleeping with the pool man?

Still staring at the ceiling, he responds to the silence:

No? Am I going too far here? Were his sexual, uh . . . ?

BONNIE

Mr Massey.

He looks down, throws up two hands.

MILES

Okay! I'm not omniscient! But my point is that he acted upon an assumption which he cannot prove and which *you* I take it deny.

BONNIE

Well . . .

MILES

Fine. That's all I needed to know. I'll take the case. It is *imperative* that I discuss matters with Oliver Olerud before we proceed any further, to work out the kinks, so to speak, in our testimony.

BONNIE

You really think we can put all this across?

Miles gives a light burbling laugh.

MILES

The truth of the matter is so self-evident to *me*, Mrs Donaly, that I'm sure I'll be able to make it equally transparent to a jury – should your husband choose to push it that far.

He rises, signalling the end of the meeting.

We'll need to caucus again to draw up a picture of your husband's worth – a map of enemy territory, so to speak. You said he's a TV producer?

BONNIE
(*rising*)
He has a soap opera, *The Sands of Time*. It's a silly show.

MILES

Well, it'll be yours soon.

They shake hands and he reseats himself as she turns to go.

BONNIE

Thank you, Mr Massey.

He waves this away and, as she leaves, is gazing dreamily out the window. He murmurs:

Still . . . you have to admire him for taking those pictures . . .

COURTROOM

We are close on the person on the witness stand, a woman in her sixties.

LAWYER
Mrs Guttman, you have testified that you were your husband's sexual slave for thirty-six years, ever since you were married –

WITNESS
Except for two years when he was in the navy, in Southeast Asia.

LAWYER
Prior to your marriage, what was your profession?

WITNESS
I was a hostess. For Braniff Airlines.

LAWYER
What is your husband's profession?

WITNESS
He manufactures staples and industrial brad-tacks. He's very successful.

We jump back to show the counsel's table in the foreground where Miles Massey chats, voice lowered, with Wrigley, a boyish, bespectacled junior associate. Beyond them we see the woman on the witness stand continuing her testimony.

MILES
I can't help it. You don't *decide* to become bored. It *happens.*

WRIGLEY
You're just looking for trouble. It's a mid-life crisis. Look, get yourself a new car.

MILES
I have a new car. I have two new cars. I'm on a tab at the Mercedes dealership.

BACKGROUND LAWYER

Couldn't you simply walk away from this abusive
relationship?

WOMAN

No, he had the videos . . .

MILES

I've torn down the house twice and I just redid the cabin at
Vail. I've got three gardeners, a cook, and a guy who waxes
my jet.

WOMAN

He would invite these girls home from the staple factory to
our condominium in Palm Springs.

MILES

My accountant keeps asking why I still go in to work.
Goddamn it, I need a challenge. This –

He waves dismissively at the courtroom.

– is not a challenge. I need something I can sink my teeth
into, professionally speaking.

WOMAN

He had a device he called The Intruder.

MILES

The problem is that everyone is willing to compromise.
That's the problem with the institution of marriage: it's
based on compromise. Even through its dissolution.

He gestures toward the background woman.

Mrs Guttman here is going to score some points concerning
her husband's sexual politics; naturally we'll try to impeach.
The process will find an equilibrium point determined by
the skill of the opposing lawyers, and then each party will
walk away with its portion of the staple factory.

WRIGLEY

That's life. Life is compromise.

MILES

No, Wrigley, that's *death*. Challenge, struggle, and of course, the ultimate destruction of your opponent – that's life. Let me ask you something: Ivan the Terrible, Henry the Eighth, Attila the Hun – what did they have in common?

Wrigley thinks.

WRIGLEY

. . . Middle name?

MILES

They didn't just win, Wrigley. They –

JUDGE

Mr Massey! I ask again if you have any questions for the complainant.

MILES

I'm sorry, your honor, I was just consulting with my associate.

He rises.

Now then, Mrs Guttman. Could you tell us who David Gonzalez is?

She looks apprehensive.

MRS GUTTMAN

Well . . . he's the tennis pro. At the club.

MILES
(*sadly*)

Ah-hah . . .

He reaches back and Wrigley puts a sheaf of pages into his hand.

And why are your letters to him addressed, 'Dear David and Goliath?'

BEVERLY HILLS STREET

It is late night, and deserted.

Engine noise approaches; headlights appear; as the car draws closer we hear singing.

It is a Mercedes convertible and as it roars by, the singing – a sloppy baritone and a giggling soprano – whooshes by with it.

We hold as another car approaches. This one is a conservative black sedan, following at a discreet distance.

PACIFIC COAST HIGHWAY

The convertible makes a hot turn onto the street and approaches with its singing.

A reverse: the car enters and roars away.

After a beat of quiet, the sedan enters and recedes.

MALIBU GUEST QUARTERS MOTEL

We are at the Malibu Seaside Cabins, which front a small motor court. The singing, squealing Mercedes screeches into the lot and rocks to a halt.

A young woman staggers out, still giggling, and holding a half-empty bottle of champagne. The driver, a middle-aged man in a tuxedo with a rumpled shirt and cocked bow tie, follows her towards one of the cabins.

As they recede, the black sedan that has been following purrs into the foreground and stops.

MOTE ROOM

The man enters and looks around. The young woman's dress has been tossed onto the bed but she is nowhere to be seen.

The man pulls an imaginary train whistle.

MAN

Choo! Choo! . . .

He looks around, in a closet, under the bed.

A female voice:

YOUNG WOMAN

Chugga-chugga-chugga-chugga . . .

The man looks, and reacts to:

A long leg poking out from behind the window curtain.

The man puffs out his cheeks in the same rhythm:

> MAN
> Ch-ch-ch-ch-ch-ch-ch-ch . . .

A salacious smile curls his lips. He draws back the curtain to reveal the young woman in red panties and a bra and a saucily cocked conductor's cap.

The man again pulls the imaginary train whistle:

> Choo! Choo!

He starts stripping off his clothes.

> YOUNG WOMAN
> Chugga-chugga-chugga-chugga . . .

> MAN
> . . . Choo! Choo!

> YOUNG WOMAN
> Pull your ears in, Rexie – you're comin' to a tunnel!

Rex lunges at the young woman and they tumble onto the bed just as –

Crash – the door is kicked open and a short stocky black man, built like a bulldog and wearing a porkpie hat, rushes into the room with a video camera glued to his eye. He looks like Clarence Thomas with a moustache.

> MAN
> I'm gonna nail your ass!!

The young woman screams, clutching the sheets to her naked bosom. Rex leaps from the bed, still clad only in his chemin-de-fer boxers, and darts around the room seeking egress.

The man with the video charges around the room, following Rex.

The video image:

Rex is stumbling around the room in a panic, looking for his clothing.

The camera swish-pans back to the young woman still screaming in the bed.

> MAN
>
> I'm gonna nail your ass!!

We swish-pan back to Rex as he bends over to pick up his trousers, mooning us.

> I'm gonna nail your ass!

GUS PETCH'S OFFICE

Pull back from video image to reveal that we are in the detective – Gus Petch's – office.

> GUS
>
> I nailed his ass.

Faintly, from the television monitor, we hear screaming and mayhem.

> WOMAN'S VOICE
>
> Trains . . .

The woman watching the monitor, Marylin Rexroth, is a cool blonde of breeding and intelligence. A diamond the size of a pomegranate is mounted on a ring on her left hand.

> MARYLIN
>
> I thought he'd outgrown trains.

> GUS
>
> They never grow up, lady. They just get tubby.

She looks at him without warmth.

> MARYLIN
>
> How charming – an aphorist.

> GUS
>
> Yeah, I've always had ample proportions. But it's all muscle – I'm hard as a rock. I'm not one of these cream-puff, sit-behind-a-desk private dicks; I'm an ass-nailer.

> MARYLIN
>
> So I see.

Faintly, from the monitor:

VOICE

I'm gonna nail your ass!

GUS

The gym four times a week, an hour and a half plus
stretching. Lifecycle. Lifestep. Lifecircuit. Gus Petch
doesn't fuck around.

MARYLIN

I must say you don't exhibit a great deal of tact for
someone in your line of work.

GUS

Look, lady, you want tact, call a tactician. You want an ass
nailed, call Gus Petch. Cripes, you look like you're takin'
it pretty good. I seen 'em carry on like Baptists at a funeral,
like they'd hired me to prove their husbands *weren't* foolin'
around.

MARYLIN

Oh, don't get me wrong, Mr, uh . . .

GUS

Petch. Gus Petch.

MARYLIN

While I don't find it terribly amusing, I *am* delighted that
you got this, uh, material. This is going to be my passport
to . . . wealth . . . independence . . . freedom.

GUS

Sounds to me like you're gonna nail his ass.

EXT. REXROTH MANSION

*Rex is trying his key in the front door of his house. Finding it doesn't
work, he rattles the knob, then leans on the doorbell.*

We hear distant chimes.

REX

Honey! . . . Honey?!

Finally, through the intercom:

> MARYLIN
> Rex, get away from the door.

> REX
> Honey, my key doesn't work – can we talk about this?

> MARYLIN
> Rex, get away from the door.

> REX
> Honey, I know you're upset, but –

> MARYLIN
> Rex, get away from the door. I don't like having to set the dogs on you.

> REX
> Oh for crying out loud, if we could – Dogs?

He looks suddenly to the right: a large Rottweiler is bounding around the corner of the house. He looks to the left: another Rottweiler.

Rex turns and runs, the Rottweilers snarling at his heels. He plunges into his Mercedes and rolls up the windows just in time. The Rottweilers lunge and bark outside the car.

Rex punches in a number on his car phone.

He looks over at the stately white Spanish hacienda as we hear Marylin coolly answering from within.

> MARYLIN'S VOICE
> Yes, dogs. I wanted some security since I'll be living here alone.

> REX
> Look, Marylin, can't we have a civilized discussion about this?

> MARYLIN
> Our lawyers can.

Bango – one of the dogs has leapt onto the hood of the car and is barking and slavering at Rex through the windshield.

REX

But honey, you know a divorce would ruin me right now.
Everything I have – everything *we* have – is tied up in my
business.

MARYLIN

Then you'll just have to sell your business, won't you, dear?

REX

The business is my entire life!

MARYLIN

Your entire life, Rex? Aren't you forgetting the Atcheson,
Topeka and the Santa Fe?

REX

Cheap shot, Marylin. You know that's just a . . . a . . . a hobby.

MARYLIN

And an expensive one. Goodbye, Rex.

REX

Honey? . . . Honey? . . . What the –

*He is looking out at the hood. The dog, though still snarling and
slavering, is oddly hunched over.*

Oh, my gosh!

The dog is shitting on the hood of the Mercedes.

LAW OFFICE CORRIDOR

Pulling Miles.

*We are tracking with him as he heads down the central corridor of
Massey, Meyerson. Walking just behind is his secretary, Doreen –
efficient, with bunned hair, referring to a small spiral notebook.*

DOREEN

You have a discovery hearing at 5:30 for the Maxine
Gopnik case –

MILES
(*absent*)
Discovery for the Gopnik . . .

DOREEN

And a Lance Kelso called – he read your article about
palimony settlements in same-sex partnerships and would
like to schedule an appointment.

MILES

Lance Kelso, same-sex . . .

DOREEN

Arthur Yardumian and his tax attorney want to reschedule
their caucus for tomorrow; Arthur had to fly to Atlanta for
a deadbeat dad hearing –

MILES

Yardumian in Atlanta . . .

DOREEN

And your 10:30 is here – Rex Rexroth.

Miles stops with an inquisitive look.

MILES

Rex Rexroth.

DOREEN

Real estate . . .

Nodding, she makes the money sign, rubbing fingers against thumb:

. . . He's okay.

MILES'S OFFICE

You may have seen it in the issue before last of World of Interiors.
Rex rises as Miles enters and greets:

MILES

Mr Rexroth.

REX

Rex, please.

MILES

Miles Massey. Please sit, relax, and consider this office *your*
office, your haven, your war room, for the duration of the
campaign.

REX

Thank you.

MILES

Not at all. Now, sir . . .

He sits into the leather executive chair behind his desk, leans back, makes a steeple of his fingers, and dons his look of deepest concern.

. . . tell me your troubles.

Rex, nervous, laughs ruefully.

REX

Jeez. Where do I start?

Miles gives an encouragingly rueful smile in return.

Well, my wife has me between a rock and a hard place.

MILES

That's her job. You have to respect that.

REX

When I first met Marylin . . . Well, we were crazy about each other. Not emotionally, of course. We just couldn't keep our hands off each other.

MILES

Mm.

REX

But then . . . But then . . .

MILES

Time marches on. Ardor cools.

REX

Yeah. So, uh . . . Well, we had an understanding . . .

MILES

Whereby . . . ?

REX

We could see other people, you know – *see* them . . .

MILES

And was this understanding documented in any way?

23

REX

No, it was just . . . understood.

MILES

I understand. Let me ask you this then, friend Rex: has
Mrs Rexroth pursued the . . . opportunities implicit in your
arrangement?

REX

I . . . I can only assume –

MILES

Not in court you can't. Has she retained counsel?

REX

I'm not sure. She has Rottweilers.

MILES

Not a good sign. And have you yourself exploited your . . .
understood freedom?

REX

There's a lady . . . a young lady . . . she lets me be myself.

MILES

Of course. And your wife is aware and/or has evidence . . .?

REX

Video.

MILES

Mmmm . . . And to cut to the chase, forensically speaking:
is there a pre-nup?

Rex hangs his head.

Miles sighs sympathetically.

The fault, dear Brutus, lies not in our stars but in ourselves.
Well, let me ask you this: what kind of settlement do you
seek? What are, for you, the parameters of the possible?

REX

Well, see, that's the problem. I can't afford to give her
anything.

MILES

Nothing?

REX

I know that sounds rough, but – I'm about to close on a deal to develop some mini-malls, and I'm mortgaged up to my heinie. If this deal goes south, I'm ruined – I'll lose millions.

MILES

So you propose that in spite of demonstrable infidelity on your part, your unoffending wife should be tossed out on her ear?

REX

Well . . . is that possible?

Miles considers.

MILES

It's . . . it's a challenge.

HEALTH CLUB

Sarah Sorkin, Ramona Barcelona and Claire O'Mara sit on a bench consulting their Filofaxes. Health club disco music plays over the public address.

SARAH

Why don't you come out to Malibu to see my new beach house tomorrow?

RAMONA

I didn't know Dmitri had a beach house.

SARAH

Neither did I until my lawyer found it. Quite a paper trail – he had it in the dog's name.

RAMONA

Hm. Well, tomorrow won't work. I'm having a body wrap. How's Wednesday?

SARAH

Hair appointment in the morning. Afternoon?

RAMONA

Shrink. How's your Thursday?

SARAH

I'm having facial injections. That kills Friday and Saturday.

CLAIRE

Botox?

SARAH

Butt fat.

RAMONA

Does that really work?

SARAH

You tell me.

Ramona stares at her with a frozen smile. Marylin Rexroth enters and exchanges air-kisses with the three women.

MARYLIN

Hello, darlings.

RAMONA

So you and Rex are . . .?

MARYLIN

Mm. As my private detective puts it, we're going to nail his ass.

RAMONA

I've been trying to nail George's ass for years but he's *so careful.*

Claire spits a little of her juice drink.

MARYLIN

Are you all right, Claire?

CLAIRE
(*hastily*)
Down the wrong pipe. Who's your lawyer?

MARYLIN

Freddy Bender. We've got a meeting this afternoon with
Rex and his schnauzer.

SARAH

Who's Rex's guy?

MARYLIN

Miles Massey.

RAMONA

Miles Massey of Massey, Meyerson?!

MARYLIN

Do you know him?

RAMONA

By reputation, and he's no schnauzer. He got Anne Rumsey
that cute little island of George's!

SARAH

George was so impressed he hired him when he divorced
his second.

CLAIRE

Muriel Rumsey.

MARYLIN

Who's she?

SARAH

Now? She's a night manager at McDonald's.

RAMONA

But Marylin, do we have a man for you!

SARAH

Thorstenson Gieselensen!

RAMONA

He just separated from his third.

SARAH

He's in fish!

RAMONA

He *is* fish!

> SARAH

Well, he's tuna.

> CLAIRE

She's keeping his name.

> SARAH

And one of his planes.

> RAMONA

And all seven children.

> SARAH

And only two are hers.

> RAMONA

But he's still tuna.

> MARYLIN

Please, ladies – I'm not seeing anyone till I've finished nailing Rex's ass.

> SARAH

But Marylin! This man is tuna!

Marylin shakes her head.

> MARYLIN

One husband at a time.

MILES'S CONFERENCE ROOM

In the middle of the Massy, Meyerson conference table is a large fruit-and-pastry plate.

Miles Massey murmurs at Rex:

> MILES

I'll do the talking. I know you'll be tempted to chime in but, remember, you're in an emotionally vulnerable state. I'm the professional.

> REX

Oh. Okay.

The door swings open. Miles rises.

MILES

. . . Freddy!

He shakes hands with the attorney who accompanies Marylin Rexroth.

. . . Freddy Bender, this is Rex Rexroth. And you are the lovely Marylin.

MARYLIN

Ms Rexroth, please. You must be Mr Massey.

MILES

Miles, please.

As they settle in:

So, Freddy, I was sorry to hear about the Goldberger award. Pastry?

Bender glares at him.

BENDER

We did very well.

MILES

Ha ha. Don't worry, Ms Rexroth, you're ably represented. I'm sure Freddy's too modest to have told you he used to clerk for Clarence Thomas. Pastry? Going begging.

BENDER

Don't try to bait me, Miles. If you've got a proposal to make, let's hear it.

MILES

Well, at this point my client is still prepared to consider reconciliation.

BENDER

My client has ruled that out.

MILES

My client is prepared to entertain an amicable dissolution of the marriage without prejudice.

BENDER

That's a fart in a stiff wind.

MILES

My client proposes a thirty-day cooling-off period.

BENDER

My client feels sufficiently dispassionate.

MILES

My client asks that you not initiate proceedings pending his setting certain affairs in order.

BENDER

Ha ha ha.

MARYLIN

Ha ha ha.

MILES
(conceding the point)

Heh heh.

REX

What's so goddamn funny?

Miles lays a hand on his arm.

MILES

Please – let me handle this.

He shoves the clipboard away and carefully studies Bender.

All right, so much for the icebreakers. What're you after, Freddy?

BENDER

My client is prepared to settle for fifty per cent of the marital assets.

Miles, who has been sipping water, gags theatrically.

MILES

Why only fifty per cent, Freddy? Why not ask for a hundred per cent? As long as we're dreaming, why not a hundred and fifty? Are you familiar with Kershner?

BENDER

Kershner does not apply.

MILES

You bring this to trial and we'll see whether Kershner applies.

REX

What's Kershner?

MILES

Please – let me handle this.

BENDER

Kershner was in Kentucky.

MILES

Kershner was in Kentucky?

BENDER

Kershner was in Kentucky.

MILES

Okay, Freddy, forget Kershner; what's your bottom line?

BENDER

The primary residence plus thirty per cent of the remaining assets.

MILES

Are you kidding?! Have you forgotten Kershner?!

Bender slams his attaché case shut and angrily stands; Miles is all innocence.

MILES

Freddy! It's a negotiation! We're all friends here!

BENDER

I'll see you at the preliminary.

Miles calls to Freddy's retreating back:

MILES

Fine! *We'll* eat the pastry.

Going through the door, Freddy doesn't react, but Marylin, following, glances back – bemused, but with a trace of a smile.

GUS PETCH'S LIVING ROOM

A group of men sit on a sofa and easy chairs drinking beer, eating potato chips, and roaring with laughter as they watch the TV. From the set we can hear distant, tinny bellows and screams.

One of the men is disgruntled.

> MAN
>
> Let's go back to the football game.

> GUS
>
> Kiss my ass!

> ANOTHER MAN
> (*to the disgruntled man*)
> It's half-time, man. This is good shit!

Faintly, from the monitor:

> GUS'S VOICE
>
> I'm gonna nail your ass!

> YET ANOTHER MAN
>
> Hey Gussie, let's see the Rabinowitz tape again.

> GUS
>
> No – wait – this is a good part here –

We hear a telephone ring.

> – she's lookin' for her panties.

The men roar with laughter.

The phone stops ringing and, after a short beat, a female voice calls:

> VOICE
>
> Gus! Miles Massey of Massey, Meyerson!

Gus is glued to the TV.

> GUS
>
> AAhh! Get a number!

32

VOICE

It's about a job tonight.

GUS

Goddamn it!

ELEGANT RESTAURANT

Miles rises from his seat as Marylin enters.

MILES

Ms Rexroth, I'm so delighted you decided to come.

The Maître D' is pulling out a chair for her.

MARYLIN

I must admit I was curious.

MAITRE D'

Something to start? Some wine, perhaps?

MILES
(*to Marylin*)

Red?

MARYLIN

French?

MILES

Bordeaux?

MARYLIN

Chateau Margaux?

MILES

'57?

MARYLIN

Mr Massey . . .

Miles nods at the Maitre D', who returns the nod and withdraws.

MILES

Your husband had told me you were the most beautiful
woman he'd ever seen, but I didn't expect the most
beautiful woman *I'd* ever seen.

MARYLIN

'Dismiss your vows, your feigned tears, your flattery,
For where a heart is hard, they make no battery.'

Miles props his chin on one fist and considers her.

MILES

. . . Simon and Garfunkle?

*A waiter appears and pours a taste of wine, which Miles sips. His eyes
on Marylin:*

'Who ever lov'd that lov'd not at first sight?'

He nods at the waiter, who pours two glasses.

Marylin smiles.

MARYLIN

Now now. You didn't ask me here to pick me up – you
could be disbarred for that.

MILES

Maybe I'm reckless.

MARYLIN

What was your performance about this afternoon?

MILES

Well . . . What did your lawyer say?

MARYLIN

Freddy thinks you're a buffoon. He says you've been too
successful, that you're bored, complacent, and you're on
your way down.

MILES

But you don't think so.

MARYLIN

How do you know?

MILES

Why would you be here?

MARYLIN

Why did you ask me?

34

MILES

Can't I be curious?

MARYLIN

About what?

MILES

Do you ever answer questions?

MARYLIN

Do you?

Flap – *a menu enters frame. It is held out to Marylin; another is handed to Miles, but he pushes it away.*

MILES

I'll have the tournedos of beef, and the lady will have the same.

WAITER

Thank you, sir.

The waiter leaves.

MILES

I assume you're a carnivore.

MARYLIN

Mr Massey, you've no idea.

MILES

Miles, please. Tell me more about yourself.

MARYLIN

All right, Miles, let me tell you everything you need to know. You may think you're tough, but I eat men like you for breakfast. I've invested five good years in my marriage to Rex. I've nailed his ass fair and square and now I'm going to have it stuffed and mounted and have my lady friends over to throw darts at it.

MILES

Mmmm . . . Man-hater, huh?

MARYLIN

People don't go on safaris because they hate animals.

MILES

So it was just a hunt – with a trophy at the end?

MARYLIN

Nothing that frivolous. This divorce means money. Money means independence. That's what I'm after. What are *you* after, Miles?

MILES

Oh, I'm a lot like you – just looking for an ass to mount.

MARYLIN

Well don't look at mine.

REXROTH MANSION – NIGHT

We are in the darkened front foyer. Gus Petch, in a black leotard, is doing stretching exercises.

He straightens up. He breathes in and out a few times very heavily, like an athlete preparing for a short heat. His hand hovers at the front doorknob.

Abruptly he twists the knob and flings himself out of doors.

EXT. REXROTH MANSION

We follow Gus's pounding feet as he runs down the drive. We hear the distant barking of Rottweilers, growing closer.

Close on Gus shows pumping arms and mouth panting.

The dogs are growing closer.

Gus is almost at the ten-foot wrought-iron front gate.

The dogs are reaching him.

He leaps – high – gets both hands wrapped around the bars. He climbs effortfully up and has managed to sling one leg over the top of the gate when . . .

. . . his half of the gate creaks slowly open.

Straddling it, Gus hinges out over the sidewalk. The dogs, wagging their tails and barking, follow him out.

Gus peers down at the slavering dogs.

GUS

Goddamn it.

NORM'S DINER — DAY

Miles and Wrigley sit at a booth in the chain coffee shop.

A large middle-aged waitress wearing a Norm's pinafore walks up to the table brandishing her check-pad.

WAITRESS

Yeah?

WRIGLEY

I'll have a salad please, uh . . .

He looks up at her.

. . . baby field greens?

The waitress stares at him.

WAITRESS

What did you call me?

WRIGLEY

I . . . I didn't call you anything!

WAITRESS

You wanna salad?

WRIGLEY

Uh, yes, uh, do you have a green salad?

WAITRESS

What the fuck colour *would* it be?

Wrigley hisses at Miles:

WRIGLEY

Why are we eating here?

The waitress looks at Miles.

WAITRESS

Whatsa matter with him?

37

MILES

Heh-heh. Bring him some iceberg lettuce and a mealy tomato wedge, smothered in French dressing.

WAITRESS

And for you?

MILES

Ham sandwich on stale rye bread, lots of mayo, easy on the ham.

WAITRESS

Slaw cup?

MILES

What the hell.

Gus Petch is sliding into the booth.

WAITRESS

How are ya, Gus?

GUS

Hello, Marge.

He slides a roll of film over to Miles.

. . . Okay, I Minoxed her address book, but don't call me any more for this penny-ante shit. I shoot action! Me and the Ikegami, Jack!

MILES

Thank you, Gus.

GUS

And those Rottweilers were a menace, man!

MILES

I told you she had dogs.

GUS

You didn't tell me they had a hard-on for Anus Africanus!

MILES

Did you see any evidence, any tell-tale signs of . . . how shall I say, any indiscretions on the part of Mrs Rexroth?

GUS

What the hell're you talking about, tell-tale signs? I see an ass, I nail it. I don't sneak around sniffin' the sheets. Goddamn it, I'm Gus Petch!

EXTERIOR

Tracking: we are outside the diner, pulling Miles and Wrigley as they cross its parking lot. Wrigley belches, then frowns.

WRIGLEY

Couldn't you be disbarred for that?

MILES

Oh, I don't think so. Maybe if I'd ordered the patty melt.

WRIGLEY

You had a guy break into her house to photograph her address book.

MILES

No no, Wrigley. I happened to let a guy know that I was *interested* in her address book. That's not criminal. I also let him know that I was taking her out to dinner, but that's not a crime either. No, I don't see myself as culpable in any sense.

He belches and hands Wrigley the film.

. . . You, on the other hand, could be disbarred for developing and examining these pictures of her address book, but that doesn't really concern me.

WRIGLEY

Right. Who am I looking for?

MILES

Tenzing Norgay.

WRIGLEY

Tenzing Norgay. That's someone she slept with?

MILES

I doubt it. Tenzing Norgay was the Sherpa who helped Edmund Hillary climb Mount Everest.

And Marylin knows him?

MILES
No, you idiot – not *the* Tenzing Norgay. *Her* Tenzing
Norgay.

WRIGLEY
I'm not sure I –

MILES
Few great accomplishments are achieved single-handed,
Wrigley. Most have their Norgays. Marylin Rexroth is even
now climbing her Everest; I want to find her Tenzing Norgay.

Wrigley belches.

WRIGLEY
But . . . how do you determine which of the people in here –

MILES
How do you spot a Norgay?

WRIGLEY
Yeah.

MILES
Well, you start with the people with the funny names.

VOICE
Oyez. Oyez. Family court for the fifth district of Los
Angeles County is now in session . . .

COURTROOM

*A large black woman in judicial robes and raiment enters from behind
the Solomonic Platform.*

The Honourable Marva Munson presiding. All rise.

*Massey, Wrigley, and Rex Rexroth in between, rise. All three stand
respectfully facing forward as they whisper out of the side of their mouths.*

REX
Have you sat before her before?

MILES

No no, the *judge* sits first. *Then* we sit.

REX

Well – have you sat *after* her before?

WRIGLEY

'Sat after her before'? You mean, have we *argued* before her before.

MILES

The judge *sits* in judgment; counsel *argues* before the judge.

REX

So, have you argued before her before?

WRIGLEY

Before *her* before, or before she *sat* before?

REX

Before *her* before. I *said* before her before.

WRIGLEY

You said before she sat before.

REX

At first I did, but then –

MILES

Look, don't argue.

REX

I'm not! I'm just –

WRIGLEY

You don't argue; *we* argue!

MILES

Counsel argues.

WRIGLEY

You appear.

MILES

The judge *sits*.

                            WRIGLEY
Then you sit.

                             MILES
That's right – or you'd stand in contempt.

                            WRIGLEY
And then *we* argue.

                             MILES
Counsel argues.

                              REX
. . . Which you've done before.

                             MILES
Which we've done before.

                            WRIGLEY
But not before her.

Crash! – *the gavel cues everyone to sit, leaving Rex standing, trying to
digest. Wrigley tugs at his sleeve:*

Rex! Sit!

LATER

*In the courtroom, now darkened, we are on a close shot of the Judge,
who sits wearing earphones, illuminated by a flickering TV monitor.*

Leaking tinnily through the headset we hear a very faint:

                             VOICE
I'm gonna nail your ass!

*At the complainant's table Marylin, also wearing earphones, weeps
demurely, knotting a handkerchief in one hand. Freddy Bender lays
a consoling hand on her shoulder.*

LATER

*Marylin Rexroth now struggles for composure on the witness stand.
She is modestly dressed and her attitude is one of shocked and
wounded innocence.*

. . . Devastated . . . I was simply devastated . . .

FREDDY BENDER

Thank you, Mrs Rexroth.

JUDGE

Mr Massey, any questions?

Miles soberly rises.

MILES

Mmmm . . .

He paces, hands clasped behind his back, affecting to be lost in thought.

Marylin, still snuffling into her handkerchief, sneaks watchful glances.

Finally Miles, still pacing, declaims:

> 'Dismiss your vows, your feigned tears, your flattery,
> For where a heart is hard, they make no battery.'

Marylin looks up from her handkerchief with a look of startled irritation. Miles stops pacing and turns to face her with a faint smile.

. . . Do you know those lines, Mrs Rexroth?

Marylin examines him through slit eyes. Freddy Bender, sensing some kind of threat, tries to head it off:

FREDDY

Objection, Your Honor!

JUDGE

Grounds?

FREDDY

Uhh . . . Poetry recitation?

MILES
(*smoothly*)

Let me rephrase. Mrs Rexroth, how high is that wall around your heart?

FREDDY

Your Honor, this is harassment! And frankly it's still a little . . .

43

He flutters one hand.

. . . arty-farty!

MILES

Rephrase! Mrs Rexroth, have you ever been in love!

Marylin hesitates, gives a 'what-does-this-mean' look to Freddy Bender. He returns a 'beats me'.

MARYLIN

Yes! Of course! With Rex!

MILES

And you've always loved him?

A smile slips out.

MARYLIN

'Whoever lov'd that lov'd not at first sight?'

Miles returns a fleeting smile.

MILES

So your sworn testimony is, you've loved Rex Rexroth since first you met?

Marylin eyes him suspiciously.

Finally, by way of answer, and of reclaiming her role as injured party, Marylin bursts into tears. She buries her face in her handkerchief and nods through the tears, helpless to speak.

Thank you, Your Honor. No further questions.

As a bailiff helps the weeping Marylin to step down:

JUDGE

Who's next, Mr Bender?

FREDDY

We rest, Your Honour.

JUDGE

Mr Massey?

MILES

Yes, Your Honor. I call Heinz, the Baron Krauss von Espy.

Heinz, the Baron Krauss von Espy!

We can hear the shout being relayed from person to person, progressively more distant, towards some outer holding room:

VOICES

Heinz, the Baron Krauss von Espy!

Wrigley, slouched at Rex's table, smugly murmurs:

WRIGLEY

. . . Tenzing Norgay.

Marylin, in the process of reseating herself behind her table, pauses stricken, mid-sob.

Freddy Bender notices and leans in.

FREDDY

Problem?

MARYLIN

Puffy!

FREDDY

Did you sleep with him?

She hisses:

MARYLIN

Don't be a fool!

A debonair man in an ascot enters the courtroom and advances to be sworn. He has slicked-back hair and the suave good looks of a Bryan Ferry or Ed Limato. He holds a small Pomeranian, who yaps as he walks.

BAILIFF

Mr, uh, Krauss, do you –

BARON

Krauss von Espy.

The dog yaps.

BAILIFF

Mr Krauss von Espy, do you –

BARON

Baron Krauss von Espy.

The dog yaps.

BAILIFF

Do you solemnly swear that the testimony you are about to give shall be the truth, the whole truth, and nothing but the truth, so help you God?

BARON

Mais bien sûr.

The judge shakes her head.

JUDGE

No maybes.

BARON

Mais *bien* sûr – but of course, yes. The Baron does not lie.

The dog yaps.

Shhh, Elsbieta. Shushy shush shush.

MILES

Now, Baron von Espy. What is your profession?

The Baron laughs airily and waves his free hand.

BARON

Silly man, I am a baron.

MILES

But uh, Baron, do you not also hold a day job, uh . . . a paying job, a square job?

BARON

Well, one has to live. I am the concierge of Les Pantelons Rouges at Bad-Gadesbourg in the Canton of Uri.

The dog yaps.

MILES

Baron, tell me, what does your job entail?

BARON

I satisfy such requests as the clientele may present.

MILES

Towels, ice, et cetera?

The Baron sniffs.

BARON

We have bellmen for that. No no, such requests that, were you at home, you would address not to your valet, but to your major-domo.

The dog yaps.

Shush, poochy-chow.

MILES

I see. Baron – do you recognise that woman?

The Baron sticks a monocle in one eye and peers.

BARON

Cher Marylin – but of course.

MILES

She was a guest at the uh, the Red uh, Trousers?

BARON

Oh, many times. For relaxing and making Alpine recreation.

MILES

I am curious about her visit of five years ago – January of 1998. Do you happen to remember any specific requests she might have had on that visit?

BARON

Yes I do.

MILES

And what did she at that time tell you she required?

BARON

She said that she required . . . a husband!

The courtroom is abuzz. The dog yaps fiercely.

47

Oh, do you want some Bonz? Does Elsbieta want some Bonz?

He looks up.

Has anyone any Bonz?

The dog still yaps. Irritated, Miles turns to the gallery.

MILES

Does anyone have any Bonz – uh, dog candies?

BARON

They are not candies! Milk Bonz! Hard crunchy bones, for the teeth!

MILES

I – we don't seem to have any – we will attend to the dog later. Now – I'm sorry –

He turns to the court reporter.

. . . Where were we?

The reporter spools up and dispassionately reads:

REPORTER

She said that she required a husband. Oh, do you want some Bonz? Does Elsbieta want some Bonz? Has anyone any Bonz? Hard crunchy bones –

MILES

Yes, thank you. Now, a husband – this is an unusual request. Did she specify what kind of husband she was looking for?

Marylin tensely prompts Freddy Bender.

MARYLIN

Freddy – stop him!

FREDDY

Objection!

JUDGE

Grounds?

FREDDY

Uh . . . hearsay?

MILES

Not second-hand, Your Honor! This is direct testimony
about the Baron's own conversation!

JUDGE

I'm going to allow it.

BARON

She said she wanted a very rich husband. She wanted to
know the businesses and the wealths – the wealths? Can
I say this, wealths?

The dog yaps.

– of our various eligible guests.

MILES

Did she have any other . . . specifications?

Freddy is desperate.

FREDDY

Objection, Your Honour! Inflammatory!

MILES

What's good for the gander, Your Honour!

FREDDY

Is this a legal argument? What's good for the gander?

MILES

Freddy, you got to show your tape!

JUDGE

Mr Massey has a point there. I'm going to allow it.

MILES

What were her other specifications!

BARON

She specificated a *silly* man!

FREDDY

Your Honour! Objection!

BARON

She specificated a man who, though clever at making money, would be easily duped and controlled!

FREDDY

Objection, Your Honour!

MILES

Shut up, Freddy, she's allowing it!

BARON

She specificated a man with a wandering peepee – how you say, a philanderer! Whose affairs would be transparent to the world!

FREDDY

Objection, Your Honour!

BARON

And finally a man whom she could herself brazenly . . .

He makes horns on either side of his head with pointing index fingers.

. . . cuckold! Until such time as she might chose to – oh, we say *fair un coup de marteau sur des fesses*, you would say, make hammer on his fanny!

The dog yaps louder. It hops frantically in the Baron's lap, nipping at his face.

Rex is purpling.

FREDDY

Objection! Irrelevant!

JUDGE

I'm going to allow it.

MILES

Tell us, Baron! Did you introduce her to such a man?

BARON

Sir! I was – the concierge!

MILES

And to whom did you introduce that calculating woman?

I introduced her to *that* silly man!

He is pointing at Rex as outrage rocks the courtroom.

The dog yaps. Freddy is on his feet.

FREDDY

Objection!

MILES

Let the record show that the Baron has identified Rex
Rexroth as the silly man!

*Rex is rising to his feet, yanking down his tie knot, swaying in front of
his chair.*

*As the dog yaps furiously the Baron rides the crescendo of noise by
loudly repeating:*

BARON

I INTRODUCED HER TO *THAT* SILLY MAN!

REX

YOU SON OF A BITCH!

Rex charges the witness box.

. . . THEY CALL ME SICK! I DIDN'T USE ANYONE!
I JUST LIKE *TRAINS*!

He wraps his hands around the Baron's throat.

I JUST LIKE *TRAINS*!

The Baron gasps through his constricted throat:

BARON

If you please, sir! Not the larynx!

The dog is in a yapping frenzy.

FREDDY

OBJECTION, YOUR HONOUR! STRANGLING THE
WITNESS!

The judge watches thoughtfully.

JUDGE

I'm going to allow it.

SORKIN MANSION

We are inside a poolhouse panning with two women whom we see outside, circling around to the front door. They are Marylin, carrying a piece of soft-sided luggage, and her friend Sarah Sorkin.

SARAH

I think it stinks. They left you with absolutely nothing! It makes you wonder about the entire legal system . . .

She opens the door and the two women enter.

. . . Like OJ.

Marylin shrugs, crossing to a bed.

MARYLIN

They bought Massey's argument: if I lied and cheated and I was only in it for Rex's money, he shouldn't have to give me any.

She dumps her suitcase onto the bed and looks around.

SARAH

That makes no sense. Why else would you put in all those years? AAAHHHH!

She staggers, clutching at her side.

MARYLIN

Sarah! Are you all right?

SARAH

I – yes – I –

Marylin steadies her and helps her to sit on the bed.

MARYLIN

What is it?

SARAH

Peptic ulcer.

She breathes heavily.

I have medication, but I can't take it before elective surgery.

MARYLIN
You shouldn't be living alone, Sarah.

SARAH
My goddamn husbands *gave* me the ulcer!

MARYLIN
But a bottle of Bromo can't love you back.

SARAH
Yeah, it's a Catch-22. I have to admit I don't like living alone. Do I really need forty-six rooms?

MARYLIN
Well, you can see people; you don't have to live like a monk.

SARAH
Ah, it's risky, palimony. That sonofabitch Marvin Mitchelson – I'm telling you, honey, getting laid is financial Russian Roulette.

She massages her stomach, looking around.

. . . Maybe I'll just tear it down, put up a cottage, twenty rooms. With my money, I can't risk fooling around. And I've got you. It'll be nice, just the girls.

MARYLIN
Thanks, but I can't sleep on your couch for ever. I'm going to marry again, and nail the guy's ass good . . .

She is gazing off, as if into the future, with a look of grim determination.

. . . and this time there won't be any . . . Puffy von Espy.

DOWNTOWN ALLEY

Marylin, in a Jill Sander original, strolls through a garbage-strewn skid-row alley. Halfway down the alley she stops in front of some garbage piled against the wall. She stares.

Two legs, barely distinguishable from the garbage, protrude from the front of the pile.

The tip of a small gilt sword protrudes from the top of the pile.

Marylin leans forward and pulls an old piece of newspaper away from the top of the mound to reveal the face of the man leaning against the alley wall. He is snoring. The small gilt sword is the top of a Daytime Television Lifetime Achievement Award.

The man is Donovan Donaly, now prematurely liver-spotted and having grown a long, ragged beard, but still clutching his award.

MARYLIN

Excuse me . . . Uh, excuse me . . . Mr Donaly?

The bum continues to snore away. She kicks him with the toe of her Manolo Blahnik and continues to prompt him as he snorfles into wakefulness:

Excuse me, Mister Donaly?

DONOVAN

In a meeting.

MARYLIN

Mr Donaly, my name is Marylin Rexroth.

DONOVAN

Tied up. Have to return.

MARYLIN

I need to speak with you now.

DONOVAN

Have you an appointment?

MARYLIN

Ah – yes. I have an appointment.

DONOVAN

I'll be there shortly.

He hawks phlegm, sits up, looks at her.

So you are . . .

He looks at his watch, elaborately focusing.

. . . my eleven o'clock?

MARYLIN

My name is Marylin Rexroth.

DONOVAN

Referred by . . .?

MARYLIN

Bunny Hartigan told me where to find you.

He looks around blearily.

DONOVAN

And where is that?

MARYLIN

I need –

DONOVAN

Did Bunny also tell you, madam, that I was not always . . .
as you see me now?

MARYLIN

Yes, up until your divorce. That's why I'm here. I –

DONOVAN

In that case, may I trouble you for the price of a bottle of
Château Grande Lafite '87, north vineyard?

MARYLIN

No. I –

DONOVAN

South vineyard?

MARYLIN

I'm sorry. I'd –

DONOVAN

'88?

MARYLIN

No. I need a –

DONOVAN

Good God, madam – what would you have me drink?

MARYLIN

Mr Donaly, you used to know a lot of people. I'll be happy
to help you, but first – I need a name.

The bum is puzzled.

DONOVAN
You led me to believe you already had one.

MILES'S OFFICE

We are close on Miles gazing through the slats of his window.

*He makes pensive popping noises with his lips. After a long frowning
beat:*

MILES
And of course we shall have to litigate. Sentence. Paragraph.

*He has raised a micro-cassette recorder to his mouth for the dictation.
After another thinking beat he continues:*

. . . Naturally the first concern for both parties is the
welfare of little Wendell Junior. Nevertheless, we question
whether the continuing expenses for his special ed. classes
are truly justified given the great strides –

A squawk box interrupts:

VOICE
Mr Massey, Mr Meyerson wonders if you have a moment.

Miles is surprised.

MILES
Herb wants to see me?

VOICE
If you have a moment.

HERB MEYERSON'S OFFICE

*Slatted shades are drawn against the sun; it is dim, gloomy. We can
just make out the shape of an ancient man – small, hunched – seated
behind an enormous desk. A gallows shape next to him is hard to
make out; it is tall, rail-thin, and fixed with a swinging, glinting
appendage.*

A voice – old, dry, rasping, lightly accented, of a long-gone Brooklyn boyhood – seems disembodied and sourceless, as if it is the voice of the gloom itself.

> VOICE
>
> Thoity-six objections sustained, tree overruled; fawteen summary judgments sought, toiteen granite; eighteen movements to void fuh respondant's prejudice, eighteen granite WHICH is a hunnut pissent . . .

An arm is being extended toward us and the glinting appendage swings with it: we see that it is an IV, which snakes down and into the hunched man's suit sleeve. The man wears oversize Swifty-Lazarre style glasses, heavily tinted in spite of the dark.

> . . . Twelve cawt days on the Rexrawt case alone; tree hunut'n twenty billable hours paralegal soivices; *four* hunnut'n two hours billable associate counsel and consultative; *six* hunnut'n eighty billable at full attorney rate and eighty-five lunches charged.

Miles takes the man's offered hand, withered and roped with veins, and accepts its clammy shake.

> . . . Counselluh, *you* are the engine that drives this foim . . .

He leans back in his chair, breathing heavily, and runs a tongue over his sandpapery lips.

At length:

> MILES
>
> Thank you, Herb.

MILES'S OFFICE

Miles sits behind his desk, fingers steepled, staring at nothing, a haunted look on his face.

His intercom squawks:

> VOICE
>
> Mr Massey –

57

MILES

Please! No calls! I'm feeling very fragile!

VOICE

I'm sorry, Mr Massey, but I felt certain you'd want to
know: Marylin Rexroth wants to see you.

MILES

Muh-Marylin Rexroth? When does she –

VOICE

She's here now.

Miles looks about, vaguely panicked.

MILES

Is she armed? – Hah-hah-hah! – Give me a minute.

MILES'S OFFICE – PRIVATE BATHROOM

*Miles runs his fingers through his hair, carefully examining himself
in the mirror.*

Suavely smiling:

MILES

Marylin! How nice to –

*He clears his throat, begins again with lower pitch, suave smile still
in place:*

Marylin! How lovely, uh . . .

*He runs a finger across his teeth, which squeak, then puts back the
suave smile.*

Marylin! What a pleasant . . .

MILES'S OFFICE

On Miles as he opens the door, suavely smiling.

MILES

Marylin, what a pleas – Who the fuck are you?

58

Facing him in the doorway is a large, roughly handsome middle-aged man in a business suit and cowboy hat.

Just behind him is Marylin Rexroth, looking as coolly beautiful as ever. She smoothly puts in:

MARYLIN

Miles, how nice of you to see us. May I introduce Howard D. Doyle of Doyle Oil?

Doyle grabs Miles's hand and enthusiastically pumps it, waggling Miles's entire body.

DOYLE

Goddamn glad ta meet ya. Marylin says you're the best, just aces.

Miles, flustered, tries to compose himself.

MILES

Er, yes, well thank you, Mr, uh – are you by any chance related to John D. Doyle of Doyle Oil?

DOYLE

Yeah, Grampa John I guess ya mean. My pop was John D. Two – the Deuce we called him; he was kinda the rebel a the family. Knocked off the whole John D. routine when he christened little ol' yours truly and Grampa nearly had a stroke. Well, a' course he *did* have a stroke, but that was later, during the labor activity in '52 when the government stepped in. They called it mediation; incipient communism Grampa John called it and that's when he had his –

MILES

Well, this is fascinating, Mr Doyle, but won't you have a seat?

DOYLE

Seat? Oh . . . thanky, don't mind if I do.

He seats himself on a couch, sinking in so that his knees are at the level of his chin.

Marylin's had me runnin' up'n down Rodeo Drive all day – kinda hit'n'run shoppin', take no prisoners, forced march

kinda thing, and brother are my dogs barkin'. We started at
the damnedest place down there near Wilshire –

MARYLIN

Yes, it's been quite a day. Miles, I know you're busy and
charge by the hour, so I'll come to the point. Howard D.
and I are planning to marry.

Miles is stunned.

MILES

Muh . . . Well, uh . . . I suppose congratulations are in
order.

DOYLE

Well, thanky Miles. Yeah, the urge to wedlock, to form a
lastin' monogamous bond sanctified by ritual, seems to be
purt nigh universal. Fact, it might innarest you to know
bein' in a related bidnis that even the native Americans –
matter of fact, I believe it was the Cree –

MARYLIN

Howard and I are here, Miles, because I have learned
through bitter experience that when it comes to
matrimonial law, you are the very best.

Miles acknowledges with a curt nod.

. . . As you are well aware, my previous marriage ended
with an unjustified stain upon my reputation. My motives
were impugned. I was slandered in court. I was painted
a harlot.

DOYLE

Aw, honey –

MARYLIN

It is therefore my desire to remove any trace of suspicion
from the mind of my dear, sweet Howard D.

DOYLE

Now, honey, I –

MARYLIN

So I wish to execute a pre-nuptial agreement.

DOYLE

I'm against it! I'm four-square, dead-set anti on this
particular –

MARYLIN

Howard's lawyers prefer it, and I *insist* upon it.

DOYLE

Aww, lawyers! No offence –

MARYLIN

Now it is my understanding that the Massey pre-nup has
never been penetrated.

MILES

That is correct. Not to blow my own horn, but they devote
an entire semester to it at Harvard Law.

DOYLE

Do they now? Course they got a helluva school up there –
we gave 'em the Doyle Building a few years back – but
I myself went to Texas A & M – that's right, I'm an Aggie.

MILES

Business?

DOYLE

No; tight end. I had a fair amount a success against the
split-T defense, 'cause when they line up all symmetrical
like that –

MILES

If I may cut in, sir –

DOYLE

Oh I don't stand on ceremony –

MILES

I just want to make sure that you *both* . . .

He eyes Marylin.

. . . understand what you're asking for here. The Massey
pre-nup provides that in the event of a dissolution of the
marriage *for any reason*, both parties shall leave it with

whatever they brought in, and earned during. No one can profit from the marriage. The pre-nup protects the wealthier party . . .

He smiles at Howard.

Without it that party is exposed – a sitting duck.

DOYLE
Hell, there ain't a lot a romance in that!

MILES
No, sir, there is not. No romance, and more to the point, no wriggle room. So . . .

His eyes are on Marylin.

. . . are we *both* sure that that's what we want?

MARYLIN
Absolutely. It's my gift to Howard for his peace of mind – whether or not it worries him at the moment.

DOYLE
Haw haw haw – Do I look worried?

ELEVATOR BANK

Marylin and Howard wait for an elevator as Miles trots out to catch them.

MILES
Excuse me, Mr Doyle, if I could just borrow your charming fiancée for a moment?

DOYLE
Hell, okay, you gonna leave a deposit? – Haw haw haw!

Miles is dragging her to the side as Doyle placidly whistles 'Turkey in the Straw'.

MILES
What're you up to?

She backs up as he tries to close the space between them.

Something you wouldn't understand. Howard D. and I are
very much in love.

MILES

I don't know what you're thinking, but I warn you: the
Massey pre-nup has never been penetrated.

MARYLIN

Thank you for your professional help.

MILES

Marylin, think of me for a moment not as an attorney but
as a friend.

MARYLIN

Does that mean you won't be billing us for this hour?

MILES

Dump him! You can't nail his ass!

MARYLIN
(*coolly*)

Is that all?

*He has backed her against the wall of an alcove which shelters a
flowering ficus.*

MILES

No, that's not all!

He kisses her.

They separate. Marylin seems amused but not displeased.

MARYLIN

I could have you disbarred for that.

MILES

It was worth it.

MARYLIN

A romantic divorce attorney.

Smiling, she walks away.

To her back:

MILES

You fascinate me.

Her tinkling laughter drifts back.

MILES'S MANSION — TENNIS COURT

*Miles Massey is jogging easily back and forth across his court,
returning balls served up to him by his tennis pro, a nubile young
woman in very short tennis shorts.*

*Miles holds a cellular phone to his ear as he covers the court, returning
volleys.*

MILES

Yes . . . All right, I suppose so . . . Yes, I'll whip something
up.

*He one-handedly flips the hinged phone closed. He tosses it to Wrigley,
who sits on a small linesman's chair by the net, wearing white cotton
boating pants, a commodore's cap, and a white T-shirt which says in
slashing red letters, 'Objection!'*

WRIGLEY

How's Lionel?

MILES

Oh, fine. He just asked me to deliver the keynote address at
this year's convention in Vegas.

WRIGLEY

That's quite an honor.

Absently, as he returns balls:

MILES

Mmm . . . I suppose.

WRIGLEY

On top of a great victory.

MILES

Oh? What was that?

64

WRIGLEY

What was that?! Rex Rexroth! He kept everything! You *won* –
no compromise. Isn't that what you wanted?

MILES

Mmm . . . I suppose.

WRIGLEY

Good God, Miles – what are you looking for?

MILES

Okay, I won, but – then what? How many cases has Herb
Meyerson won?

WRIGLEY

The old man? More than anybody. He's a legend.

MILES

And look at him. Eighty-seven years old, still the first one
into the office every day; no home life –

WRIGLEY

Who needs a home when you've got a colostomy bag?

MILES

No wife, no family – Wrigley, she can't really love this dope,
can she?

WRIGLEY

Who? Who loves who?

MILES

Marylin Rexroth signed a pre-nup with an oil millionaire.

WRIGLEY

A *Massey* pre-nup?

MILES

Yeah . . .

WRIGLEY

'Only love is in mind if the Massey is signed.'

We hear guitar music. From behind the bower, bearded Father Scott emerges, strumming his guitar and singing.

>   FATHER SCOTT
> Parsley sage, rosemary and thyme,
> Remember me to one who lives there . . .

A pullback reveals Howard D. Doyle in a white suit and cowboy hat before the altar with Marylin.

> . . . She once was a true love of mine.

The last arpeggiated chord rings out; birds tweet, everyone sits.

As Miles and Wrigley seat themselves Wrigley is weeping; Miles is irritated.

>   MILES
> What the hell is wrong with you?

>   WRIGLEY
> I can't help it. Even with the business we're in, I . . . it gets me every time.

>   MILES
> Is she going through with this, Wrigley? I can't believe she loves this stiff. I can't believe she's going through with it. Is she going through with this?

As the crowd quiets with the end of the song, Wrigley murmurs:

>   WRIGLEY
> If she's not going through with it, she's cutting it awful close.

>   FATHER SCOTT
> Thank you all for coming to this celebration of the love between our two friends, Marylin and Howard.

Beaming, he inclines his head to each of them.

> Marylin, Howard, you are about to embark on a great journey, a journey of love and caring and joy. In today's cynical world it's so hard to take that great leap of faith

aboard the ship of love and caring. But today Marylin and Howard are taking that leap, and telling us, their friends, that they *do* believe, that they *do* have faith, that they *do* love. They stand on the poop deck that is Commitment, next to the taffrail that is Understanding, by the bos'un who is . . . who is, uh, who is also at the taffrail. And they are waving to us. Are they waving bon voyage, or are they bidding us follow, in our own vessels of love, joy and caring? Think about it . . .

There is silence, broken only by the twitter of birds and Wrigley's snorfling.

Finally:

Do you, Howard Drexler Doyle, take Marylin to be your shipmate on this voyage through life, through gale and doldrum, seas choppy, wild and calm?

HOWARD

I do, Father Scott.

FATHER SCOTT

And do you, Marylin Rexroth, take Howard to be your shipmate and companion, be it in first class or in steerage, to ports of every clime?

MARYLIN

I do.

MILES

Argh!

Heads turn. Miles bites a knuckle. Birds twitter.

FATHER SCOTT

Then, by the power vested in me by the State of California, I now pronounce you man and wife.

Wrigley bursts into tears.

A kiss. Cheers. Applause.

WEDDING RECEPTION

A reception on the grounds of the Beverly Hills Hotel.

Father Scott strolls through the crowd strumming his guitar and singing.

FATHER SCOTT

I am just a poor boy,
His story seldom told;
I have squandered my existence . . .

Miles is darkly brooding as Wrigley opens a Tiffany box to show him the contents.

WRIGLEY

What do you think?

MILES

What are they?

WRIGLEY

Berry spoons.

MILES

Spoons.

WRIGLEY

Berry spoons. Everybody has *spoons.*

MILES

And nobody *needs* berry spoons.

WRIGLEY

Everybody likes berries!

MILES

What're you, Pollyanna? Where did you see those things, anyway, in a Martha Stewart catalogue? Next to the silver napkin rings? The stadium-seat ass-warmers? Good God, Wrigley, how many cockamamie material possessions do we have to amass –

WRIGLEY

Miles – why so angry?

Ding ding – *Howard is tapping a Bowie knife against his wine glass. The crowd quiets.*

HOWARD
Ladies and gentlemen, boys and girls: I know it's not common practice for the groom to give his bride a gift on their weddin' day. But folks, ever since I met Marylin I just can't seem to stop giving her things . . .

There is a smattering of applause.

. . . and I don't want to stop!

More applause.

. . . 'cause it feels s'durn good!

Applause and laughter. Howard D. turns to one side to address Marylin, taking her hand between his paws as she beams up at him.

Darlin', like the padre said, I want there to be love and trust between us, love and trust and nothin' else. Now I'm not too big on words –

Laughter from the gallery.

Well, okay, I *am* big on words, but I'm also big on deeds. And thisahere deed is just to show ya – Aw shucks, honey . . .

He reaches into his breast pocket and withdraws a piece of paper.

. . . Bring out the barbecue sauce, Chow Sing!

A Chinese man in a chef's outfit comes out and places a plate and a bowl of barbecue sauce in front of Doyle. Doyle is knotting a bib around his neck.

This is for you, darlin'!

He starts tearing strips off the piece of paper, dipping them in the barbecue sauce, and eating them. His mouth stuffed with paper, Doyle repeats:

Thish izh for you, darlin'!

The crowd is murmuring – the murmurs grow in volume – a smattering of applause – cheers – more applause – wild cheers.

Slowly, rhythmically, Miles starts thumping his hands together, nodding comprehension.

> MILES
>
> Brilliant. Brilliant.

Wrigley is puzzled.

> WRIGLEY
>
> What is it? Miles, what is it?

Miles's hand-clapping accelerates.

> MILES
>
> Brilliant. It's the pre-nup. IT'S THE PRE-NUP! BY GOD, IT'S BRILLIANT!

Wrigley's eyes widen. He looks back up at Doyle eating the paper, barbecue sauce dribbling down his chin.

> HOWARD
>
> This is for you, darlin'!

Wrigley bursts into tears.

> WRIGLEY
>
> That's . . . the most romantic thing . . . I've ever seen . . . in my LIFE!

> HOWARD
>
> THISH IZH FOR YOU, DARLIN'!

LATER

Marylin stands at the punch bowl accepting congratulation. Miles approaches and draws her aside.

> MILES
>
> I'd like to offer my congratulations. That was a beautiful gesture of Howard's.

> MARYLIN
>
> Howard is a beautiful person – a diamond in the rough.

> MILES
>
> And I have a feeling that someday soon you'll be taking that diamond and leaving the rough.

MARYLIN

In a month or two. As soon as I've established that I tried
to make the marriage work.

MILES

May I offer my services?

MARYLIN

Thanks, but I'm going to retain Freddy Bender. Poor
Freddy; he was a little blue after my last divorce.

MILES

I admire your loyalty – to lawyers, anyway. I guess without
the pre-nup this will be something even Freddy can manage.
But how did you get Howard to do it? It seemed like he
thought it was his own idea.

MARYLIN

Oh, Mr Massey, surely you've addressed enough juries to
appreciate the power of suggestion.

MILES

Mm. Look – now that your marriage is winding down –
have dinner with me.

MARYLIN

Oh no. Nothing doing until the ink is dry on the
settlement.

Massey smiles.

MILES

This will be no settlement. If I know Marylin Rexroth, this
will be total and complete annihilation.

We hear a distant rumble as of approaching thunder.

With a roar we cut to:

LEAR JET COCKPIT

*A uniformed pilot and co-pilot are cruising the corporate jet high
above a vast ocean of clouds. The pilot is wearing a headset. After
a long moment of listening he shakes his head.*

PILOT

Jesus . . .

CO-PILOT

What . . .?

PILOT

I've heard some . . . I've heard some sick things . . . in my –

CO-PILOT

What?!

The pilot reaches above his head and throws a small toggle switch and the cockpit is awash with the sound of screaming, laughter and music:

MALE VOICE

Oh Casey Jones was the rounder's name,
'Twas on the 6:02 that he RODE to fame!

LEAR JET CABIN

Screaming with laughter, two naked damsels in conductor's caps are pushing Rex Rexroth around the cabin on a miniature locomotive. He is wearing his railroad boxers and bellowing 'The Ballad of Casey Jones'.

COCKPIT

CO-PILOT

Who *is* that guy?

PILOT

Rex Rexroth, the mini-mall king. Getting to be the richest man on the West Coast, from what they say.

The co-pilot shakes his head.

CO-PILOT

Jesus.

FROM THE SPEAKER

Hup! Come all you rounders if you wanna hear . . .

CO-PILOT

Why're they going to Muncie?

The pilot shrugs.

PILOT

He's thinking of buying Indiana.

EXTERIOR

Whooosh – the plane roars away.

EXT. CAESAR'S PALACE

A huge, alabaster, classically proportioned male head – neck – muscular shoulders – torso. It is the great oversized David outside of Caesar's Palace. Just before our continuing boom down brings David's groin into frame, a foreground sign intervenes:

NATIONAL ORGANIZATION OF MATRIMONIAL ATTORNEYS, NATIONWIDE – WELCOME UNTO CAESAR'S.

INT. CAESAR'S PALACE

A tracking shot follows Miles as he walks down a row of slot machines, inserting a coin into each one and pulling its arm. Wrigley follows with a little plastic bucket, collecting the winnings as each successive machine pays off.

MILES

You know why I can't stand Las Vegas, Wrigley?

WRIGLEY

Why's that?

MILES

The emptiness. The isolation. The dacronization of the moral fabric. *You* know what I mean.

WRIGLEY

Oh sure. 'The dangling conversation; the superficial sighs.'

MILES

You tell me, Wrigley: has Las Vegas democratized marriage – or cheapened it?

He glances back at the bucket. After a beat Wrigley sheepishly reaches into his pocket, pulls out a few quarters and tosses them in.

. . . You see, people get to Vegas and all of a sudden the rules of the moral universe don't apply. If God is dead, all things are possible. Why, I saw an ad in the paper here – 'No-fault divorce – two-week divorce without a lawyer.' It made me sick to my stomach. 'No-fault divorce'? Good God, talk about an oxymoron. What's the world coming to?

WRIGLEY

One man can only do so much.

MILES
(*momentarily irritated*)

What the hell're you talking about. Freddy!

He gestures hello to Freddy Bender, who is crossing the floor to the elevators.

WRIGLEY

I had lunch with Freddy Bender yesterday. He tells me that Marylin Rexroth-Doyle is now richer than Croesus.

MILES

Ah, but is she richer than *Mrs* Croesus.

WRIGLEY

She could buy and sell *you* ten times over.

MILES

My God – is that her?

Indeed it is: Marylin Rexroth-Doyle is strolling across the gaming floor in a chicly casual outfit and leading an impeccably groomed show-quality Afghan hound.

WRIGLEY

Mm. Freddy said she was flying in with him. Celebrating, I guess.

MILES

I'm fascinated by that creature. She deserves every penny. They pay great athletes a king's ransom; well, Wrigley, look at *her* – an athlete at the peak of her powers.

He grabs the coin bucket from Wrigley.

Excuse me.

WRIGLEY
You stay away from her, Miles. Take a cold shower and
recite your keynote address.

*But Miles trots away, jingling, toward the elevators. He slips in with
Marylin and the Afghan just as the doors are closing.*

MILES
You're looking well, Marylin. Obscene wealth becomes you.

MARYLIN
Oh, hello, Miles. I guess I should've known you'd be here.

MILES
Be here – I'm the keynote speaker!

MARYLIN
How nice for you.

MILES
'Whose Community Property Is It Anyway? Nailing Your
Spouse's Assets.'

MARYLIN
Excuse me?

MILES
My speech.

MARYLIN
I'm sure it'll bring the house down.

MILES
It's an easy crowd. At this point you're probably the only
person I can't teach anything to.

MARYLIN
Mm.

MILES
Correct me, but – since by now the ink must be dry,
I believe I have the right to collect.

On . . .?

MILES

You promised to have dinner with me once you were free.

MARYLIN

I said that I wouldn't while I wasn't, which implies no promise once I am.

MILES

Noted. Let me rephrase . . .

He reaches down to pat the Afghan.

I would be delighted, honored even, if you would –
AIEEEAIEEEE!

The Afghan has Miles's hand clamped in its jaw.

Coolly:

MARYLIN

Howard.

The dog placidly drops the hand.

Miles rubs it.

MILES

Cute. Named after your ex?

Marylin shrugs.

MARYLIN

I'm sentimental. Well, I have no plans this evening. I suppose a little dinner couldn't do any harm.

FANCY RESTAURANT

We move in on one of the tables where Marylin and Miles sit as a waiter pours them champagne. The Afghan, Howard, sits patiently beside them.

WAITER

La Veuve Clicqout Ponsardin, 1982.

Thank you. I'll take care of it.

As he fills Marylin's glass:

You know, Marylin, this is a moment to savor. Okay, we were adversaries, but we're also professionals: let's raise a glass in friendship.

He raises his glass; she raises hers.

MARYLIN

To victory.

They clink and drink.

MILES

So how does it feel?

Marylin cocks an enquiring eye. He elaborates:

Victory? Independence?

MARYLIN

Ah. Yes.

She looks down at her drink.

Well, frankly, Miles . . .

The thought drifts.

MILES

Mmm . . . Not everything you'd hoped for, huh? I know the feeling.

MARYLIN

Independence is a two-edged sword. A friend of mine – my best friend – Sarah Sorkin?

She looks interrogatively at Miles, but he shrugs.

Sarah Battista O'Flanagan Sorkin?

Miles nods.

MILES

The O'Flanagan settlement.

MARYLIN

Mm.

MILES

Heh-heh.

Marylin remembers it too:

MARYLIN

Heh-heh-heh. Anyway, three fine settlements, more money than she could ever hope to spend, her vaunted independence and . . .

MILES

Yes. Don't tell me. She sits around the house, afraid to see people, afraid of putting her portfolio in play.

MARYLIN

And only a peptic ulcer to keep her warm at night.

MILES

Mm. Yes, at a certain point you achieve your goals, and –

MARYLIN

– find out that you're still not satisfied.

MILES

Mm. Well – should we order?

MARYLIN

Yes, I – well, I'm not really . . .

MILES

Not hungry, huh? Neither am I.

A long, pensive moment.

*Miles reaches across the table and takes her hand. She lets him.
He strokes it.*

CAESAR'S PALACE ELEVATOR

*Miles and Marylin stand side by side. The only sound is the hum of
the rising car, punctuated by the* ding *of each passing floor.*

26TH FLOOR HALLWAY

Symmetrical in two directions, the hall stretches away from the elevator bank.

Miles takes Marylin's hand.

> MILES
> Marylin —

She puts a finger to his lips.

Sadly, Miles relinquishes her hand.

She walks away, growing smaller and smaller down the endless hallway. Miles watches her go.

NIGHT SKY

Clap of thunder, bolt of lightning. Distant, echoing wails.

HERB MEYERSON'S OFFICE

A woozy Dutch rack along a pointing suitcoated arm.

> SANDPAPERY VOICE
> Eighteen hunnut billable hours . . . twelve hunnut'n twenty-one motions tuh void . . .

The woozy track finds the cadaverous hand at the end of the arm with an IV tube swinging from it. There are more wailing voices.

> . . . five hunnut'n sixty-faw summary judgments . . . a hunnut'n twenty-nine thousand four hunnut'n seventeen lunches charged . . .

Ring! Ring! Ring!

CAESAR'S PALACE — MILES'S ROOM

He bolts up in bed, sweating.

Ring!

He gazes stuporously about, reaches for the ringing phone.

                              MILES
Hello?

                         MARYLIN'S VOICE
Miles?

                              MILES
Hello? Marylin?

                         MARYLIN'S VOICE
Sarah Sorkin just died.

MARYLIN'S ROOM

*Miles bursts through the door, wearing his Caesar's Palace bathrobe
over his pyjamas.*

*Marylin, weeping, is also in a Caesar's Palace bathrobe. Howard, the
Afghan, rests his head dolefully in her lap.*

                              MILES
Marylin!

He embraces her. She continues to weep, blubbering:

                            MARYLIN
Her ulcer . . . perforated . . . infection . . .

                              MILES
There, there.

                            MARYLIN
. . . Peritonitis . . . Miles –

                              MILES
What, Marylin?

                            MARYLIN
She was alone – she'd been . . . dead . . . two days when her
. . . pilates instructor found her!

Miles is grim-faced.

                              MILES
Marylin, listen to me.

                               80

He takes her hand, looks into her eyes.

No arguments! No discussion! I'll have Wrigley meet us at the Wee Kirk o' the Heather!

EXT. WEE KIRK O' THE HEATHER

A taxicab screeches to a halt.

WEE KIRK O' THE HEATHER — RECEPTION

Miles and Marylin, both still in their Caesar's bathrobes, burst in.

Wrigley, in a suit and holding a briefcase, has been waiting.

> MILES

Wrigley!

> WRIGLEY

The vows are from an Arapaho dawn-greeting ceremony, the music is Simon and Garfunkel, and *this* . . .

He pulls a paper from the briefcase.

. . . is the Massey pre-nup.

An old man at the reception counter wearing a tartan tam sizes up the party, presses both hands down on the countertop, and barks:

> OLD MAN

You the two gettin' married?

Wrigley murmurs apologetically:

> WRIGLEY

Mr MacKinnon here will be officiating . . . Sorry . . . short notice . . .

> MILES

Pen.

Wrigley hastily pulls a ballpoint from his pocket and clicks it. Miles grabs the pre-nup and, as he turns to Marylin, his tone softens:

Dear, you're welcome to examine this; it's the Massey pre-nup which, as you know, is iron-clad –

WRIGLEY

I tried to reach Freddy Bender –

MILES

We tried to reach Freddy Bender to have him here for your protection as well –

WRIGLEY

Couldn't get him.

MILES

– but we couldn't get him.

OLD MAN

Are you two here to get married or to bullshit!

Miles glares at the old man.

MILES

Sir! Please!

Marylin has taken out her glasses and is reading the pre-nup, murmuring:

MARYLIN

If, for any reason . . . dissolution . . . party of the first part . . . all right.

She signs it.

MARYLIN

Now you can't hope to benefit from the marriage.

Miles looks at her solemnly.

MILES

Not in any way.

MARYLIN

My wealth is completely protected.

MILES

As if a lead veil had been drawn across it.

MARYLIN

And you still want to marry me?

MILES

More than ever.

Wrigley bursts into tears.

OLD MAN

Are ye rentin' kilts!

CHAPEL

Miles and Marylin stand before the altar. Miles and Wrigley are wearing blazers and kilts. Marylin is wearing a tam and a tartan shawl.

An organist sedately plays the Hawaiian War Chant.

The Old Man consults a clipboard as he conducts the ceremony.

OLD MAN
Do you, uh, Miles Longfellow Massey of Massey, Meyerson, Sloan and Gurolnick, LLP, take Marylin Hamilton-Rexroth-Doyle, to be your lawful wedded wife, to –

MILES
I do, yah I do, uh-huh –

OLD MAN
Let me finish!

He glares at Miles.

Jesus! Have ya never been married before!

Chastened, Miles bows his head.

. . . to have and to hold, to love and to cherish, till death do ye part?

A long beat, through which Miles stares at his shoes.

Marylin nudges him.

MILES

I do.

OLD MAN

And do you, Marylin Hamilton-Rexroth-Doyle, take Miles
Longfellow Massey of Massy, Meyerson, Sloan and
Gurolnick, LLP, to be your lawful wedded husband, to have
and to hold, to love and to cherish, till death do ye part?

MARYLIN

I do.

OLD MAN

I now pronounce ye man and wife.

*There is the skirl of bagpipes as Mrs MacKinnon, an elderly woman
in tartan, pipes and marches down the aisle, one slow goose-step at a
time.*

Wrigley blubbers.

CAESAR'S PALACE — HONEYMOON SUITE

*A magnificent heart-shaped bed sits on an elevated platform, looking
out over the rippling lights of the Las Vegas strip.*

A swathe of light cuts the floor as we hear the door being kicked open.

*Miles enters, still wearing kilts, staggering under the weight of
Marylin, whom he carries.*

He deposits her on the bed and kisses her.

She responds at first, and then stops. Something is troubling her.

Miles looks at her. Hesitantly:

MILES

Marylin?

MARYLIN

No. No. This is wrong.

MILES

Is it the kilt?

MARYLIN

Miles – do you love me?

MILES
More than anything.

MARYLIN

Can I trust you?

MILES

You can trust me.

She rolls over, gropes in her purse, pulls out a folded paper, and rips it in half.

Miles looks at it, slack-jawed.

Dear . . . you're exposed!

MARYLIN

A sitting duck.

They stare at each other.

Miles lunges and kisses her passionately. She responds with equal passion.

We tilt discreetly up to the twinkling lights of the Vegas strip. A distant marquee sizzling with chase lights promises 'Corbett Monica, Oct. 8–10.'

We hear the distant pounding of a gavel.

CAESAR'S PALACE — BANQUET HALL

Bang – *the gavel hits a block.*

SECRETARY

I hereby declare the twelfth congress of the National Organization of Matrimonial Attorneys, Nationwide . . . open!

He bangs the gavel once again amid murmurs from the large assembly of divorce lawyers, mostly trim men in their forties in expensive Italian suits.

As our first order of business, it is my privilege to call to the podium our keynote speaker who is none other than the Society's president: from the Los Angeles firm of Massey,

Meyerson, Sloan and Gurolnick, please welcome a man whose name is synonymous with bitter disputes and big awards . . . Miles Massey!

There is a genuinely warm hand as Miles makes his way to the podium. He is dressed in last night's rumpled formalwear; he is unshaven, tousle-haired and baggy-eyed; but in spite of his hungover appearance, he has a glow.

He fishes a sheaf of papers from his breast pocket.

MILES

Thank you, Secretary Bombach. And thank you, ladies and gentlemen . . .

He looks down at his speech.

In the world of . . .

He stares at the paper, thinks.

. . . in the world of matrimonial law, there are multiple tactics . . .

As he again pauses to consider, there is murmuring in the crowd. At length Miles picks up the sheaf of papers and, slowly and deliberately, tears it in half.

More murmuring. Miles looks out at the crowd.

Friends. This morning I stand before you a very different Miles Massey than the man who addressed you last year on 'The Disposition of Marital Assets Following Murder-slash-Suicide' . . .

He pauses to master his emotions.

I wish to talk to you today, not about technical matters of law. I wish to talk to you about something more important. I wish to talk to you from the heart. Because today, for the first time in my life, I stand before you naked . . . vulnerable . . . and in love.

More murmuring.

. . . Love. It is a word we matrimonial lawyers avoid. Funny, isn't it – that we are frightened of this emotion, which is in

86

a sense the seed of our livelihood. But today Miles Massey
is here to tell you: love need cause us no fear. Love should
cause us no shame. Love . . . is good.

*In the audience a couple of matrimonial lawyers exchange puzzled
looks. There are scattered coughs. People do not like the drift of these
remarks.*

Now I am of course aware that these remarks may be
received with cynicism. Cynicism – that refuge of the weak,
the selfish, the emotionally paralysed. Cynicism – that
cloak which advertises our indifference and drives away all
human feeling. Cynicism – that suit of armor which we
poor frightened combatants put on to approach the bar.
Well I am here to tell you that that Cynicism, which we
think protects us, in fact destroys – destroys Love, destroys
our clients, and ultimately – destroys ourselves.

He pours himself a glass of water; considers.

Colleagues! Let me ask you a question. When our clients
come to us confused, angry, hurting because their flame
of love is guttering and threatens to die – should we seek
to extinguish that flame, so that we can sift through the
smoldering wreckage for our paltry reward? Or should we
fan this precious flame – this *most* precious flame – back to
loving, roaring life? Should we counsel fear or trust? Should
we seek to destroy – or to build? Should we meet our
clients' problems with Cynicism – or with Love?

The audience stares.

The decision, of course, is each of ours. For my part, I have
made the leap of love, and there is no going back. Ladies,
gentlemen, this is the last time I shall address you as the
president of N.O.M.A.N. – or as a member . . .

Murmurs.

I intend to devote myself hereafter to pro bono work in
East Los Angeles, or wherever I am needed. Thank you . . .
and may God bless you all.

He steps down.

There is dead silence as he makes his way across the dais, his shoes squeaking on the wooden floor.

Somewhere a lonely cough echoes.

Miles reaches the stairs at the end of the podium and starts descending.

Someone at the back of the banquet hall starts to clap slowly, uncertainly.

Someone else joins him.

There is a small scattering of slow applause.

Miles has reached the floor and is starting up the center aisle.

The applause is growing.

One clapping man rises to his feet.

More join him. The applause is growing louder, faster.

One man on the aisle reaches out and thumps Miles on the back.

MAN

Thank you, Miles . . .

The applause swells.

The entire audience is on its feet. Everyone near the aisle reaches out to lay a congratulatory hand on Miles.

The audience is roaring.

Miles is mobbed.

He catches someone's eye. The applauding crowd parts.

Wrigley stands staring at Miles; he is stunned; his mouth hangs open.

There is a moment of suspense between the two men.

Finally Wrigley throws open his arms.

WRIGLEY

I love you, man!

He rushes Miles.

They embrace.

The crowd roars.

HALLWAY

Wrigley is hurrying Miles away from the banquet room. Distantly we can still hear the roar of the crowd. Tears stream down Wrigley's face.

> MILES
> So, Wrigley, I'll be relinquishing my partnership in Massey, Meyerson. If you would like to join me in my new endeavors I would be delighted to have you.

COCKTAIL LOUNGE

They are entering a cocktail lounge off the casino floor. As they approach the bar we hear a television announcer:

> ANNOUNCER
> We return now for the conclusion of today's episode of *The Sands of Time.*

> MILES
> Of course I can't offer you the kind of financial remuneration that you've grown accustomed to, but the work will have its own rewards – BARKEEP!

> TV CHARACTER
> The patient is suffering from acute myocardial infarction – we have to operate!

Wrigley, looking up at the television, tugs at Miles's sleeve.

> WRIGLEY
> Hey, this is the soap that used to belong to Donovan Donaly . . .

> MILES
> You'll be serving in a junior capacity, of course –

ANOTHER TV CHARACTER
Shouldn't we call in a specialist from Mass General?

WRIGLEY
Say, Miles, isn't that – isn't that –

MILES
As you know in any firm there can be only one ramrod –

Miles has turned to glance up at the bar TV.

It shows Howard Doyle, dressed in the pale-green hospital scrubs of a daytime TV surgeon. His rube accent and buffoonish air are gone; he endows his character with a dignified intensity:

DR HOWARD
Good God, man, we can't wait for a specialist. Look at her upper left ventricle – that infarct is dynamite!

SECOND DOCTOR
But Doctor, you're new here – it would be your very first procedure here at Saint Ignatius and – she's your daughter!

DR HOWARD
Let me tell you what they called me in medical school: Mackenzie the Mechanical Marvel . . .

He solemnly regards his own hand as he flexes it.

I've got no nerves.

WRIGLEY
He's . . . he's . . .

He and Miles gaze up at the TV.

. . . an actor. *Not* an oil tycoon. An actor. So Marylin . . .

He sifts through the implications.

Golly, she has no money. She's . . . she's . . . poor.

He looks down at Miles.

Well, thank God you have the pre-nup.

Miles stares back.

MILES

I have no pre-nup.

Wrigley nods and thoughtlessly echoes:

WRIGLEY

You *have* no pre-nup.

Miles nods in turn:

MILES

I have no pre-nup.

Wrigley finally grasps it.

WRIGLEY

. . .YOU HAVE NO PRE-NUP?!

Miles stares mutely back, his eyes wide with horror. His mouth stretches open.

MILES

AAAAAAAAAHHHHHHHHHHHHHHHH!

WRIGLEY

AAAAAAAAAHHHHHHHHHHHHHHHH!

HALLWAY

Miles is fighting against the current in a sea of humanity coming out of the banquet room. He is oblivious to the claps on the back from the lawyers who pass him; he is searching for someone.

LAWYER

You're beautiful, man!

LAWYER 2

We just dissolved the Society!

LAWYER 3

By acclamation!

MILES

FREDDY!

He shoves two lawyers out of the way, grabs Freddy Bender by the lapels and shoves him up against the wall.

I'm going to see that you get disbarred! Prosecuted! Thrown into jail!

FREDDY

Take your hands off me, Massey.

MILES

You just wait until I –

FREDDY

I've done nothing illegal or unethical.

MILES

You lied! You lied! You said Howard Doyle –

FREDDY

They were married, they were divorced; there were no assets. Everything on the up and up. His accent was phoney, but I'm aware of no law against that.

MILES

Aahhh!

Miles releases him.

Why did she do it, Freddy? Why?

Freddy pulls down his sleeves and brushes down his suit.

FREDDY

That's attorney–client privilege. Marylin has retained me to pursue an action in which I believe you will figure as respondent.

As the surging tide of lawyers starts to bear him away, Freddy looks back over his shoulder.

Sorry, Massey. But as a great and clever man once said, what's good for the goose . . .

*Miles storms in past a bellman who is leaving loaded down with bags.
The room is made-up, empty, and sterile. Marylin is just putting some
items into a toiletry case, about to leave.*

As Miles enters, Howard, the Afghan, growls.

MARYLIN

Oh hello, Miles.

Miles's anger has evaporated; he is now ruined, disconsolate.

MILES

Back to Los Angeles?

MARYLIN

Yes. I think it's only fair to warn you: after a decent interval
I plan to have Freddy seek an injunction that will forbid
your approach within five hundred feet of my house.

MILES

Meaning my house?

MARYLIN

I believe the residence will be part of the settlement.

MILES

Did last night mean anything to you?

MARYLIN

Oh, about the same as it'll mean to you – half of your net
worth.

She smiles at his wounded look and softens.

You'll always be my favorite husband, Miles.

MILES

Marylin – please –

MARYLIN

But no more sentiment, darling . . .

She gives him a peck on the cheek.

I really *have* to be going; the dog is rented.

She leaves.

Miles sits dejectedly on the bed, staring at the dog, who has remained behind and who, oddly, is making a snarling face at him as he hunches over.

Marylin calls crisply from the hallway:

> . . . Howard!

The dog straightens up and bounds away, tail wagging, leaving a pile of shit on the thickly piled rug.

Miles stares, haunted, at the pile of shit.

MILES'S MANSION — POOL AREA

Marylin and Sarah Sorkin are stretched out in deckchairs on the deck by Massey's pool. Marylin's two Rottweilers are also there, one of them snoozing in the sun, the other with its head resting adoringly on Marylin's feet. The outdoor stereo speakers play Piaf singing 'Non, je ne regrette rien' as both women gaze contemplatively at the sparkling surface of the pool.

Marylin is holding a fruit-and-rum drink, Sarah a glass of Pepto-Bismol. After a long beat:

SARAH

But you're going through with it.

MARYLIN

Yes, yes, it's just that I felt sorry for him, for a minute there. At the preliminary hearing he seemed so . . . *beaten.*

SARAH

Well, he *is* beaten! Fair and square!

MARYLIN

Yes, but –

SARAH

Aw, that pathetic look, that's what they fall back on when they don't have a pre-nup. Just stay strong until the divorce is final. Relax and enjoy your pool.

Silence. Edith Piaf. Lapping water.

> MARYLIN
>
> Do you think he's eating enough?

> SARAH
>
> Marylin!

HERB MEYERSON'S OFFICE

Close on a bag of fluids.

We pull back from the milky, yellowish bag of fluid to show that a nurse is unhooking it and removing it from under Herb Meyerson's wheelchair, where it collects drainage.

She places it up on the IV gantry and connects it, and swaps the now empty drip under the wheelchair to collect drainage.

The gloomy office's venetians are, as always, drawn, making Herb a dark, enigmatic figure.

> HERB
>
> This woman has humbled, shamed and disgrazed the entire foim.

A reverse shows Miles in front of Herb's desk, with Wrigley cowering behind him.

> MILES
>
> Yes, Herb.

> HERB
>
> Counselluh, this foim deals in powuh. This foim deals in p'seption. This foim cannot prospuh . . . nor long endoowa . . . if it is p'seeved as dancin' to the music . . .

He waves his free arm to the beat of music unheard.

> . . . of the hoidy-goidy.

> MILES
>
> I understand. Herb . . . I just . . . for the first time in my career . . . I don't know what to do. I'm a patsy . . . A sitting duck. I'm lost.

HERB

Lost! I'll tell you what you can do, you can –

He brings himself up short and turns to the nurse.

Leave us.

She heads for the door. As Wrigley tries to slither out with her:

Not you, counselluh!

Wrigley, whimpering, returns.

You can act like a man. Let me tell you sumpn, smart guy. You tawt you had it all figgud out. Trust. Marriage. All ya goddamn love love love. Well now you lissena me. I'm gonna talk to you about the goddamn LAW!

He climbs unsteadily to his feet and tries to pace, gesticulating, with the IV swaying dangerously behind him.

We *soive* the law! We *honuh* the law! We make our goddamn bread'n *buttuh* by the law! And sometimes, counselluh, we *obey* the law . . .

He pauses to let this sink in.

. . . but, counselluh . . . this is not one a those times.

CLAM HOUSE

An enormous gangster sits into close-up. He is perspiring heavily through a green silk shirt. His mouth hangs open and he breathes through it with the rasping wheeze of an asthmatic.

His labored breath rattles as he stares across the table at someone off. At length, a voice:

VOICE

Are you Wheezy Joe?

Still staring, but perhaps by way of answer, the gangster raises an inhaler, sticks it in his mouth, and squeezes: whush.

GANGSTER

Which a youse is Smith?

A reverse shows Miles and Wrigley seated across a small round table in the seedy low-lit clam house. Photos of Ted Kennedy and the Pope adorn the walls.

MILES

Uh . . . We're here representing Mr Smith, on a . . . on a matter of some delicacy.

GANGSTER

Who's the pigeon?

MILES

Excuse me?

GANGSTER

Who ya want me to kill?

Miles and Wrigley exchange nervous glances.

MILES

Well, we – uh, that is to say *Mr Smith* – would like to uh, neutralise a, uh, terminate, uh – render into a state of, uh, you know, so she isn't so much, uh . . .

WRIGLEY

. . . breathing . . .

MILES

. . . a certain, uh, business associate by the name of Marylin Rexroth-Doyle-Massey – uh, Smith – uh, Massey.

GANGSTER

Is that . . . *one* person?

MILES

Here's her picture . . .

He shoves an envelope across the table.

. . . and the address where she's staying. It's the residence of a Mr Massey. Uh, Smith. Uh, Massey. It's, uh, Mr Smith's house. Though Smith himself is not involved.

WRIGLEY

Because of an impending legal action we need this to happen within a certain . . . time-frame.

On an expedited basis.

The gangster stares expressionlessly. He raises the inhaler again and, with his eyes still on the two men, squeezes: whush.

GANGSTER

. . . You're in a rush.

WRIGLEY

Mr Smith is, yes.

All three men stare.

A long beat.

Miles explodes:

MILES

She won't suffer, will she?

He bites a knuckle, gazing fearfully at the gangster.

The gangster stares impassively back.

GANGSTER

Not unless you pay extra.

REXROTH MANSION — PULLMAN ROOM

It is an enormous oak-panelled room. It is furnished with chairs, sofas, and a huge circular bed upholstered in crimson crushed velvet. A coal fire roars in the far corner. On the wall above the bed a film loop is being projected: soft-core pornographic images, oddly intercut with vintage-train footage — locomotives of various types, trains pulling into stations and crossing majestic landscapes, signalmen in overalls waving lanterns, etc.

On the bed, Rex is surrounded by six naked beauties smeared in coal dust and wearing conductors' caps. They dance around him as he jumps up and down in his boxers.

REX

I'VE BEEN WORKING ON THE RAILROAD . . .

TARTS

All the livelong day!

> REX
>
> I'VE BEEN WORKING ON THE RAILROAD . . .

> TARTS
>
> Just to pass the time away!

> REX
>
> CANTCHA HEAR THE WHISTLE . . . the whistle . . .
> AAAAWWWWWWWWWWWW . . .

Rex hunches over, clutching his left arm.

One by one, the girls stop dancing and stare. There is a somber silence, broken by another:

> AAAAAAAAWWWWWWWWWWWW . . .

The girls are all watching now.

One of them steps forward.

> TART
>
> Whatsa matter, Rexie?

WRIGLEY'S APARTMENT

The living room. In the foreground someone is sleeping on the couch. Empty liquor bottles litter the coffee table in front of him.

We hear a phone ringing in a different room. It rings several times.

The figure on the couch stirs, rolls over, moans, clamps a pillow over his head.

The ring of the distant telephone is interrupted and we hear a muffled voice:

> VOICE
>
> Hello? . . . Yes, he's here. Just a minute . . .

We hear approaching footsteps and Wrigley enters the background, knotting a bathrobe. He turns on the light in the living room. In a voice fraught with worry and curiosity:

> . . . Miles. It's for you.

The figure on the couch pulls away the pillow. It is indeed Miles Massey. He blearily takes the offered phone.

MILES

Hello . . . Yes . . . What?! . . . Yes . . . I see . . .

After another listening beat he drops the phone away. He stares dully into space.

My God.

WRIGLEY

What?

MILES

That was Marvin Untermeyer.

WRIGLEY

Yes?

MILES

He was Rex Rexroth's personal attorney.

WRIGLEY

Ye . . . 'hat do you mean, *was*?

MILES

Rex just had a massive coronary. In the middle of a business meeting. He's dead.

Wrigley is mildly puzzled.

WRIGLEY

Well – I'm sorry to hear that. But you weren't close, were you?

MILES

Marvin says that Rex's will is four years old. He never redrafted it.

WRIGLEY

Yes?

Miles's voice is still flat, inflectionless:

MILES

Everything goes to Marylin.

He looks up at Wrigley.

They stare at each other.

A long beat.

Suddenly:

> # AAAAAAAAAAAAAAAAAAHHHHHHHHHHHHHHH!

> WRIGLEY
> # AAAAAAAAAAAAAAAAAAHHHHHHHHHHHHHHH!

MINUTES LATER

*Wrigley is consulting a small notebook; Miles paces with the telephone.
He punches numbers with the thumb of the hand holding the phone;
his other hand holds a coffee cup from which he takes trembling slurps.*

> WRIGLEY
> . . . oh-seven-oh-six!

Miles mutters as he punches in numbers:

> MILES
> . . . seven-oh-six. That's only six digits!

> WRIGLEY
> Oh-OH!

> MILES
> Seven-oh-six-oh?

> WRIGLEY
> Oh-seven-oh-six!

> MILES
> Oh-seven-oh-six.

He starts re-punching the numbers.

> WRIGLEY
> She's *not* poor! She's richer than you. No pre-nup. She's
> exposed! She's the sitting duck!

> MILES
> Sitting duck! Yes! Can't kill her! No need!

WRIGLEY

It would be pointless. She's exposed!

MILES

Exposed! Pointless – AHHH!

WRIGLEY

What?

MILES

Ringing! It's –

We hear an answering machine pick up. There is labored breathing, and then:

VOICE

You have reached Wheezy Joe. Wuddya want?

There is more labored breathing and then a beep.

Frantically:

MILES

Joe! This is Mr Mass – Mr Smith! On Smith's behalf! Speaking on my own behalf, this is to instruct you it's no go! Do you understand me?! No go on Marylin! This comes directly from Smith!

WRIGLEY

Although you acknowledge no association!

MILES

I – that's right! I acknowledge no association! In connection with this whole affair which is now NO GO! But I believe these would be Smith's wishes. Speaking without knowledge.

He slams down the phone.

. . . You think I'm protected?!

WRIGLEY

That was good!

MILES

Am I protected?!

WRIGLEY

I think that would hold up!

MILES

Marylin!

WRIGLEY

Marylin, yes!

MILES

What do we do? What if he's –

WRIGLEY

Yes! Yes! Marylin!

MILES

If he's on his way there?!

WRIGLEY

He's – Yes! Marylin! We, uh, we, uh, we, uh, we, uh . . .

MILES'S MANSION

We are looking at the house through the windshield of a car. On the dash in the foreground are a bottle of Revive! auto air cologne and a small statuette of the Virgin Mary. From out of shot, we hear the familiar whush.

The reverse shows Wheezy Joe lowering the inhaler from his mouth. He picks up an automatic handgun and screws a silencer onto the barrel.

Back to the view of the house: we hear the car door open and slam shut. A moment later Wheezy Joe appears, shambling up the walk to the front door.

WRIGLEY'S CAR

Wrigley drives, speeding, taking corners hard, still in his bathrobe. Next to him Miles, wind whipping his pajamas, punches numbers into the car phone and mumbles:

MILES

Get her out, buy some time; get her out, buy some –

MILES'S MANSION — BEDROOM

In a darkened bedroom the phone starts ringing.

WRIGLEY'S CAR

As before.

> MILES
> – out, buy some time –

BEDROOM

The ringing phone.

Finally a hand enters to pick it up. We follow the hand up to reveal an unperturbed:

> MARYLIN
> Hello?

WRIGLEY'S CAR

Miles bellows into the phone:

> MILES
> Marylin! You must leave the house immediately! It is imperative that you –

We intercut Marylin in her bedroom.

> MARYLIN
> Miles?

> MILES
> Yes! It is imperative that you –

> MARYLIN
> Oh, please, Miles, pending final settlement, my entitlement to use of the house is quite clear –

> MILES
> No! You don't understand –

MARYLIN

And in fact Freddy's restraining order forbids you to even call me. So unless there's some kind of emergency –

MILES

Yes! That's it! An emergency!

WRIGLEY

An emergency!

MARYLIN

What do you mean? What is it?

MILES

It's – it's – it's . . . a gas main! Leaking! I just remembered I left on the gas main, which leaks!

MARYLIN

Leaking gas?

MILES

A deadly colorless odorless liquidless gas that . . . that . . . that . . . that attacks the central nervous system and causes diarrhoea and facial tics!

MARYLIN

Well – why don't you call the gas man?

MILES

Gas man? Like to! Should! Want to! Can't! Can't call the gas man! Pinned down! Can't get to a phone!

MARYLIN

You can't get to a phone?

MILES

Camping! I'm camping! Wanted to call the gas man, but there's a bear outside my tent!

WRIGLEY

Brown bear!

MILES

Brown bear!

MARYLIN

Who's there with you?

MILES

No one! Wrigley! Also camping – and refuses to make a
break for it! Heh-heh – You know Wrigley! So you must
leave the house! Immediately! Very dangerous!

MARYLIN

You can't get to a phone to call the emergency gas man
because you and Wrigley are pinned down by a bear so –

MILES

Brown bear!

MARYLIN

– brown bear, so you called me up to warn me.

MILES

Exactly! Yes! It's complicated!

MARYLIN

Well . . .

MILES

We've, uh, left some things out for, uh, legal reasons but it's
dangerous. Leave the house!

He disconnects.

I think she bought it.

WRIGLEY

Good. We're good. What now?

MILES

We, uh – when we get there we just wait! She'll have left;
we wait for Wheezy Joe, we tell him it's No Go!

WRIGLEY

Good plan! Good plan!

MILES

It's done – we're protected – I think she bought it!

WRIGLEY

Good plan!

BEDROOM

Marylin has cradled the phone and is looking at it thoughtfully.

She walks slowly around the room, pausing at the mantelpiece to pick up a framed picture of Miles, which she contemplates.

We pan with her continued walk to bring Wheezy Joe into frame. He stands with his back pressed to the wall, hands raised in surrender, the two Rottweilers in front of him at snarling attention.

> MARYLIN
>
> Who sent you?

> JOE
>
> Mr Smith.

She shows the picture of Miles to Wheezy Joe.

> MARYLIN
>
> Is this Mr Smith?

> JOE
>
> No . . .

She cocks an eye at him.

> . . . that's his lawyer.

> MARYLIN
>
> Well, whatever they're paying you, I'll double.

> JOE
>
> Who's the pigeon?

We faintly hear a car screeching to a halt.

EXT. MILES'S MANSION

Massey and Wrigley pile out of the car, still dressed in their pajamas. Each clutches an aerosol canister of 'Mailman's Friend' pepper spray.

> MILES
>
> Careful. Rottweilers.

INTERIOR

We hear a key scrape in the lock. The front door swings open in a dark foyer as Miles and Wrigley tiptoe in.

MILES

I think she's gone. I think she bought it.

WRIGLEY

Good stuff! This place is empty!

MILES

Except for the Rottweilers!

WRIGLEY

Sure! Rottweilers!

MILES

You go that way.

They split up, each reconnoitering an opposite direction.

Kitchen:

Miles tiptoes in, looking warily about. He backs towards the swinging doors connecting to the dining room.

Dining room:

Wrigley tiptoes through, looking warily about. He backs through the swinging doors connecting to the kitchen.

He and Miles face each other mid-door.

AAAAAAAAAAAAAAAAAAHHHHHHHH!

WRIGLEY

AAAAAAAAAAAAAAAAAAAHHHHHHHH!

Ssssssssssss – *they spray each other with 'Mailman's Friend'.*

MILES

AAAAAAAAAAAAAAAAAAAHHHHHHHH!

WRIGLEY

AAAAAAAAAAAAAAAAAAAHHHHHHHH!

They run – into each other, and then push each other away.

108

We follow Miles, who twists across the floor, gasping for breath, rubbing at his face, until – thump!

He has run into a large human chest.

> MILES

AAAHHH!

The chest belongs to Wheezy Joe. Miles, still agitated, pats Wheezy Joe appreciatively on the chest.

Wheezy Joe! Thank God you're in time! *You're* not in time! *We're* in time! Thank God we're in time!

Wheezy Joe stares at him.

It's no go! Don't you get it? No one any the wiser! Okay!

He makes cow-herding motions with his hands.

You can go home now! Goodbye! Thanks so much!

Wheezy Joe is taking earplugs out of his pocket.

No no! No contract! It's all over! No go!

This has no effect on Wheezy Joe, who is twisting the earplugs into his ears. Miles is exasperated.

Wrigley! Will you explain it to this lunkhead! No go! It's all over!

Wrigley shoves his face into Wheezy Joe's, who has reached into his pocket and taken out his gun.

> WRIGLEY
> (*helpfully*)

No go! No go!

> MILES

We'll settle your contract later!

> WRIGLEY

Golden parachute!

> MILES

Don't you get it?

WRIGLEY
Here's what happened, Mr Carnera –

MILES
It's all off! Look – you're fired! *Tornare a Sorrento! Adios, amigo!* It's – it's – Oh my God!

Wheezy Joe is raising the gun at him.

Miles sprays him with Mailman's Friend.

Bang! – *Wheezy Joe fires blindly, scrunching his eyes against the chemical, sucking for breath like a jet engine revving for take-off.*

Miles and Wrigley duck and scurry.

Bang! – *Wheezy Joe is rampaging around the room, still firing, thumping at his chest with his free hand for his inhaler.*

Bang! – *Still firing, he pulls out the inhaler but blindly bobbles it.*

Miles and Wrigley scurry around, vainly seeking egress.

Wheezy Joe reaches with his gun hand to keep the inhaler from falling. He momentarily bobbles both gun and inhaler.

Miles pops up in front of him.

Wheezy Joe recovers and raises the gun to his mouth as he points the inhaler at Miles.

He squeezes – whush – *Miles squints against the asthma mist and lets out a horrified:*

WHEEZY JOE!

Bang! *The gun's report is followed by the sound of a body dropping heavily to the floor.*

Silence.

Wrigley comes over to stand next to Miles. The two men look sadly down at the floor.

WRIGLEY
We *told* him it was no go . . .

You may have seen it in the same issue of World of Interiors *that featured Miles Massey's office, or else earlier in this movie during the Kershner discussion. A fruit-and-pastry basket lanquishes on the middle of the table.*

Wrigley sits bouncing the steepled fingers of one hand against the other, tunelessly humming.

> WRIGLEY
>
> Dum-dum-duh-dum-duh-dum . . .

Miles sits gazing sadly out the window.

The room is otherwise empty.

There is the whirr of ventilation.

The click of the door attracts both men's attention and brings them to their feet.

Marylin walks in, chic, calm and beautiful as ever, followed by Freddy Bender, who sits next to her, places his attaché case on the tabletop, and snaps its clasps.

> FREDDY
>
> Gentlemen.

> WRIGLEY
>
> Freddy.

Miles and Marylin are looking at each other. Quietly:

> MILES
>
> Hello, Marylin.

> MARYLIN
>
> Hello, Miles.

> MILES
>
> This . . .

He has trouble bringing out the words.

> This is where we met. Remember?

MARYLIN

Of course I remember.

Miles sadly shakes his head.

MILES

Hard to believe that when you go through that door today,
you'll be leaving my life for ever.

MARYLIN

It's not something *I* wanted either.

MILES

But then – I guess – something inside me died when
I realized that you'd . . . hired a goon to kill me.

MARYLIN

Wait a minute – *you'd* hired him to kill *me*!

FREDDY

Now you *both* wait a minute! Nobody hired anyone to kill
anyone!

WRIGLEY

Hear, hear.

There is uncomfortable shifting in seats. Freddy looks at Marylin.

FREDDY

Apparently, from what I can gather, a burglar broke into
your house –

WRIGLEY

Miles's house!

FREDDY

Whatever! A burglar broke in, intending to loot the place,
repented, became despondent over his life-style, and shot
himself.

Miles is still looking at Marylin.

MILES

Where does that leave you and me?

FREDDY

We've outlined a settlement . . .

He pushes a piece of paper across the table.

We think it's generous.

Miles ignores the paper, which lies unclaimed on the middle of the table.

WRIGLEY

My client is prepared to consider a reconciliation.

Marylin looks at Miles.

MARYLIN

How could I trust you, after . . . all of this?

FREDDY

Well, that's exactly right. The point here is that flagrant bad faith has been dem –

Miles, staring at Marylin, cuts in:

MILES

You wounded me first, Marylin. I'm not proud of what I've done. But God knows – I did trust you once – and if you gave me a chance . . .

FREDDY

Heh-heh – If you'll pardon me, I think my client is well beyond the point of considering any –

MARYLIN

But how can I trust you, Miles? How could I ever really . . .

Slowly, with his eyes still on Marylin, Miles reaches into his suit coat. He withdraws a piece of paper, spreads it flat on the table in front of him and, still gazing at her:

MILES

You know there's nothing in the Massey pre-nup that says it can't be executed *after* the parties wed.

He decisively clicks the button on a ballpoint pen, looks down at the paper in front of him, and scribbles his name.

He pushes the paper across the table toward Marylin.

Gazing at him, seeking the truth in his eyes, she absently picks up the paper.

There is a long silence. We hear only the hum of ventilation, and Wrigley's quiet snuffling.

Freddy is looking down his nose through his glasses, over Marylin's shoulder, at the sheet of paper. She, however, looks only at Miles.

FREDDY

Well. If this is indeed the Massey pre-nup – and a cursory examination tends to suggest that it is – then we *withdraw* our proffered settlement and there's nothing left to disc . . . aaahh!

Marylin has just ripped the Massey pre-nup in half.

Wrigley sobs openly.

Freddy stares at the torn paper.

My God – Marylin! You're exposed!

Miles rises slowly to his feet.

He puts his knuckles on the tabletop and leans forward.

Marylin rises slowly to her feet.

She leans forward.

They kiss.

Wrigley, now sobbing loudly, abruptly snuffles to a stop, noticing something:

Freddy Bender has each half of the torn pre-nup pinned to the table with an index finger and is furtively dragging them along the tabletop towards himself.

WRIGLEY

COUNSELLOR!

He leaps to his feet and – whack – slams his hand down to trap the document – too late –

Freddy has grabbed it away. He scoops it into his attaché case, which he hugs to his chest as he scuttles around the table.

Wrigley pursues him out the door.

Miles and Marylin slowly separate, gazing at each other.

> MILES
> Did you hear something?

> MARYLIN
> Only the patter of little lawyers' feet.

> MILES
> Where did you find Howard Doyle?

> MARYLIN
> The actor? Oh, through a TV producer – I think you know him. I gave him an idea for a new show, so he made me a partner.

They kiss again.

> MILES
> I guess that means *I'm* a partner.

> MARYLIN
> I guess it does.

As he leans in for another kiss:

> MILES
> What exactly is it that we're partners in?

TELEVISION STUDIO

An announcer cups one ear and calls into a microphone:

> ANNOUNCER
> Good evening, ladies and gentlemen, and welcome to *America's Funniest Divorce Videos*. And here's the star of our show, Gus . . . PETCH!

The studio audience roars.

Gus Petch trots out from behind a curtain to riotous applause. He is wearing a Botany 500 blazer and his porkpie hat.

GUS

You're goddamn right, folks, my name is Gus Petch and we got a great show for ya. We're gonna make ya laugh, we're gonna make ya cry, and most of all . . .

He waves one fist in a circle over his head, leading the audience in a roaring:

GUS AND AUDIENCE

We're gonna NAIL . . . YOUR . . . ASSSSSS!!!

The show's theme music strikes up as the house monitors show crude hand-held videos of sinning couples.

The producer, wearing headphones, gives big, two-handed upward waves to the audience to cue louder cheers, clapping his hands to encourage them to do likewise, and energetically pointing at a flashing applause sign. It is Donovan Donaly.

Photo Section